# LEE

★ THE | GENERALS ★

# LEE

## A Life of Virtue

★ THE | GENERALS ★

## John Perry

THOMAS NELSON
Since 1798

NASHVILLE   DALLAS   MEXICO CITY   RIO DE JANEIRO

Published in Nashville, Tennessee, by Thomas Nelson. Thomas Nelson is a registered trademark of Thomas Nelson, Inc.

Thomas Nelson, Inc., titles may be purchased in bulk for educational, business, fund-raising, or sales promotional use. For information, please e-mail SpecialMarkets@ThomasNelson.com.

Scripture quotations are from the King James Version.

**Library of Congress Cataloging-in-Publication Data**

Perry, John, 1952–
    Lee : virtue in action / John Perry.
       p. cm.
    Includes bibliographical references.
    ISBN 978-1-59555-028-6
    1. Lee, Robert E. (Robert Edward), 1807–1870. 2. Generals—Confederate States of America—Biography. 3. Confederate States of America. Army—Biography. I. Title.
E467.1.L4P47 2010
973.7'3092—dc22
[B]                                               2010016322

*Printed in the United States of America*

10 11 12 13 14 WRZ 5 4 3 2 1

*To Robert Thomison, for forty years a*
*true and faithful friend, and a Southern*
*gentleman who has held fast to the best of the*
*old while embracing the best of the new*

# Contents

# A Note from the Editor

To CONTEMPLATE THE lives of America's generals is to behold both the best of us as a nation and the lesser angels of human nature, to bask in genius and to be repulsed by arrogance and folly. It is these dichotomies that have defined the widely differing attitudes toward the "man on horseback," which have alternatively shaped the eras of our national memory. We have had our seasons of hagiography, in which our commanders can do no wrong and in which they are presented to the young, in particular, as unerring examples of nobility and manhood. We have had our revisionist seasons, in which all power corrupts— military power in particular—and in which the general is a reviled symbol of societal ills.

Fortunately, we have matured. We have left our adolescence

with its gushing extremes and have come to a more temperate view. Now, we are capable as a nation of celebrating Washington's gifts to us while admitting that he was not always a gifted tactician in the field. We can honor Patton's battlefield genius and decry the deformities of soul which diminished him. We can learn both from MacArthur at Inchon and from MacArthur at Wake Island.

We can also move beyond the mythologies of film and leaden textbook to know the vital humanity and the agonizing conflicts, to find a literary experience of war which puts the smell of boot leather and canvas in the nostrils and both the horror and the glory of battle in the heart. This will endear our nation's generals to us and help us learn the lessons they have to teach. Of this we are in desperate need, for they offer lessons of manhood in an age of androgyny, of courage in an age of terror, of prescience in an age of myopia, and of self-mastery in an age of sloth. To know their story and their meaning, then, is the goal here and in the hope that we will emerge from the experience a more learned, perhaps more gallant, and, certainly, more grateful people.

Stephen Mansfield
Series Editor, *The Generals*

# Introduction

ROBERT E. LEE has been one of the most misunderstood figures in American history for a hundred and fifty years. Who he was and what he stood for are still controversial because the scars of the Civil War remain tender six generations after the last shot was fired. We even argue today over whether to call it the Civil War (implying a nation divided) or the War between the States (meaning two nations). Questions linger over so basic a point as what the fighting was all about. Why did Americans shed one another's blood so savagely for four terrible years? Why did we fight the deadliest war in our history on our own soil against our own brothers? The typical history textbook will tell you that it was all about slavery. Yet the same source omits the facts that President Lincoln campaigned on a platform of not interfering with slavery anywhere it was already legal, that not all slave states joined the Confederacy, and that only about 10 percent of the white population in the South actually owned slaves.

These books, and the generations of Americans who've read them, will say that Robert E. Lee fought to preserve slavery. During his lifetime and today, Lee has been accused of defending the indefensible, of going to war to uphold laws that allowed one man to own another the same way he might own a chair or a set of dishes. He appears to be a wealthy slave master who turned against his own nation to defend the rich and leisurely lifestyle of the Virginia plantation class, which depended on slave labor.

Northern newspapers branded Lee as a traitorous lowlife who was "following in the footsteps of Benedict Arnold," the notorious Revolutionary War turncoat. Lee never denied these slurs that sprang up early in the war and follow him to the present day. He never fought back against his slanderers because he was too busy fighting on the battlefield. Besides, he was such a humble man he wouldn't have done it anyway. And since he never tried to shape his own historical legacy, his enemies shaped it for him, tarring him down through the years with the brush of slaveholder and turncoat.

The truth about Robert E. Lee, gleaned from his own words and the events of his life, is exactly the opposite. Lee consistently condemned slavery as unnatural, ungodly, impractical, economically flawed, and wrong. He probably never owned a slave in his life. Based on the sketchy documentation that survives, he may have inherited four slaves from his mother's estate, but evidently he gave them their freedom within a month. His wife inherited nearly two hundred slaves when her father died, but they were all freed within five years, as her father had directed in his will. By the time Lincoln's government enacted the Emancipation Proclamation on New Year's Day 1863, there were no slaves left on the Lee family property to be freed by it. Following the spirit of the law as well as the letter, Lee tracked down as many runaway slaves as he could and had their letters of manumission delivered to them.

Lee believed without question that slavery was a moral outrage. Yet like most Southerners who shared his view, he accepted the institution because he didn't know how to deal with the practical obstacles to emancipation. How would millions of blacks with no education and no property mix with a white society that had held them in bondage for more than two hundred years? Would they flood the labor market and drive down wages, causing an employment crisis for better-paid white workers? Would centuries of pent-up resentment explode into a slave revolt? Lee believed that the problems of institutionalized slavery would be solved, and that slavery would eventually be phased out in God's good time. He was confident that the abolitionists would reach their goal by being patient and practical a lot sooner than they would by forcing proclamations and ultimatums down Southern throats. Lee categorically and repeatedly condemned slavery. He never endorsed it and never fought for it.

He *did* fight for the right of individual states to make their own laws except in matters where the Constitution specifically gave power to the federal government. Even as a hero of the Mexican War who had been a commissioned officer in the U.S. Army all his adult life, Lee felt a stronger sense of loyalty to Virginia than to the nation as a whole. He was a Virginian first and an American second. This position sounds shocking to modern readers until they consider the historical perspective. When Lee graduated from West Point in 1829, the United States in its final form under the Constitution of 1789 was only forty years old, while Virginia had existed for more than two centuries. The Lee family roots were deeply planted in Virginia soil long before a United States was even an idea.

Today the national government is so much a part of our daily lives that it's hard to imagine how strong the individual states once were and how determined many Americans were to keep them that way. U.S. senators were elected not by the voters but by powerful state legislatures. The Constitution prohibited direct taxation of the people by the federal government. Much of the nation's money, and much of the responsibility for governing, remained with governors and their cabinets. America's founders had worked and argued for years to come up with a system to unite states for their common good in areas like interstate transportation and national defense, yet leave them independent otherwise.

Lee recognized and respected this balance, but his love for his native state trumped everything. He left the U.S. Army because he saw a time coming when he would have to lead soldiers to keep states in the Union by force. That would mean bearing arms against another Virginian, which he would never do. In letters and conversations during this time, Lee explained repeatedly that he acted only to protect Virginia's right to make its own laws and set its own policies as guaranteed by the Constitution. The most contentious and emotional conflict in the states' rights debate was whether Congress could dictate states' policies on slavery. This incendiary issue has generated a confusing smoke screen down through the years, leading millions of history students to accept the false notion that slavery, not states' rights, was Lee's motivation for joining the Confederacy. Actually he didn't even join the Confederacy after he resigned his commission. Lee headed the Virginia state militia, not a Confederate army, because Virginia had voted not to join the Confederate States of America (CSA). Later, after the state changed its position, the militia was absorbed into the Confederacy, and Lee took command of CSA troops. For Lee, the shift had nothing to do with supporting whatever the Confederacy stood for and everything to do with serving Virginia regardless of its policies or political affiliations.

American voters and policy makers had fought over slavery in the context of states' rights for decades before the Civil War. As early as 1819, when John Adams and Thomas Jefferson were still alive, the issue threatened to divide the young nation. Congress and the states avoided civil war then by tamping down the argument with the Missouri Compromise of 1820. This legislation divided the vast Louisiana Purchase into a northern part, where new states could not have slaves, and a southern part, where they could. An important distinction here is that the new southern states wouldn't automatically become slave states, but could if they chose to. The compromise was modified several times, then finally declared unconstitutional in 1857. Deciding the case of *Dred Scott v. Sandford,* the Supreme Court ruled that Congress had no right to outlaw slavery in the federal territories, and that slaves were not citizens, but property. Slaves could not sue, and like any other piece of property, they could not be taken from their owners without due process.

In the end, the Missouri Compromise only delayed the bloody

tragedy of America dividing against itself. It may actually have fed the fires of division by establishing a geographical dividing line, reinforcing the North versus South tensions that finally boiled over in 1861. One wise scholar who takes neither side in the fight believes America was destined to split regardless of states' rights, slavery, or anything else. Raimondo Luraghi taught American history at the University of Genoa in Italy. In his book *The Rise and Fall of the Plantation South*, he writes that even during the colonial period, the American colonies were two separate cultures with separate interests. The South, he says, was settled by Renaissance gentlemen who loved learning, the land, and fine clothes and houses, and put their wealth in property. By contrast, colonists in the North were Puritan businessmen who loved commerce, business, and thrift, and put their wealth in gold, silver, stocks, and bonds.

To suggest that the Civil War happened for any reason other than abolishing slavery is to risk being called an apologist, a promoter of the "lost cause," or worse. What matters here, though, is not what textbook writers think, or what Signore Luraghi or anybody else thinks, but what Robert E. Lee himself thought. Lee consistently affirmed that slavery was wrong, but at the same time he believed that Virginia had the unassailable constitutional right to decide the question without federal interference.

Lee's devotion to Virginia and his historic association with the Southern cause often obscure the fact that he was also one of the great patriots in American history. Heroism was in his blood. Robert's father, Henry "Light Horse Harry" Lee, was a Revolutionary War hero who fought beside George Washington and was honored with a gold medal for his leadership on the battlefield. Later he was governor of Virginia and a member of Congress. Lee's father-in-law, George Washington Parke Custis, was Martha Washington's grandson and grew up at Mount Vernon as Washington's foster son. The Custis estate, which Lee's wife inherited and where the Lee children were raised, was filled with treasures and mementos of Washington's life. From his earliest years then, Lee was surrounded by reminders of the Washington legacy, and he had a strong sense of responsibility to uphold it.

Part of Lee's determination to serve his nation, his state, and his family honorably came from the fact that his father failed so spectacularly in the end to do these things. Despite his military and political triumphs, he was a lifelong spendthrift whose financial troubles went from bad to worse while Robert was still a boy. Hounded by creditors, the former war hero eventually served time in debtors' prison. Further misery awaited him after his release, as a consequence of his opposition to war with England in 1812. Defending a friend who published an anti-war newspaper, Lee was attacked by a mob and left for dead. Permanently disabled and disfigured, financially destitute, Light Horse Harry abandoned his wife and children for Barbados, leaving young Robert to care for his invalid mother, help raise his siblings, and manage the household as best he could.

At the age of eleven, Robert took up the responsibility his father left behind. As a boy he was unusually mature and capable, always compassionate, always reliable. From these traits sprang the devotion to duty and honor that was the driving force in his life. It made him an exemplary son, a distinguished cadet at West Point, and a dedicated officer in the Corps of Engineers. It also gave him the patience and humility to do his work diligently and well. Lee spent eighteen uneventful years as an officer before making a name for himself during the Mexican War in 1847. Following the march toward Mexico City, he was commended for "greatly distinguished" service. The American general in chief, Winfield Scott, later called him the finest soldier he had ever seen. Marked at last as a rising star, Lee transferred to the cavalry, and be led U.S. forces against the slave rebellion at Harpers Ferry, Virginia, in 1859. One of Lincoln's first actions as president was to commission Lee as a colonel. Soon afterward, the president offered Lee command of seventy-five thousand troops being raised as a deterrent to any states considering secession.

Lee turned down his commander in chief not because he was unpatriotic, not because he favored slavery, but because he would not raise his sword against a fellow Virginian. Lee was a methodical and intelligent man who surely knew that, barring a miracle, the South was doomed to defeat from the outset. The North had about three times the population of the Confederacy and vastly more of everything needed to wage war, from blankets to locomotives. But he saw the choice as a matter of honor, and for that he was willing to sacrifice everything.

Who, then, was the real Robert E. Lee? How did he become the man he was? How is the genuine article different from the myth? These are the questions this book proposes to answer.

The aim here is not to shape Lee's historical image, but to clear away the misleading encrustations of the past, the assumptions and misinformation, to reveal the man behind that image. The man who, as a student, patiently carried his mother in and out of her carriage because she was too weak to walk. Who, years later, considered it his special honor to push his invalid wife in her wheelchair. Who declared that the sight of two dozen little girls dressed in white at a birthday party was the most beautiful thing he ever saw. Who, weary from the burdens of battlefield command, took time to pick wildflowers at dawn and press them into a letter for his family. Who inspired starving, shoeless soldiers to keep fighting beyond their endurance. Who believed in honor enough to give up everything else to preserve it. A warrior who wanted nothing but peace. A devoted Christian who spared nothing to live as he believed Christ wanted him to live.

But why does it matter who Robert E. Lee was anyway? It matters because Robert E. Lee was a great man and his example has much to teach us. To know how he lived, what he thought, and what experiences and legacies defined his life is to know the essence of honor, sacrifice, faith, humility, and ultimate triumph in the face of devastating defeat. As much as the world has changed in a hundred and fifty years, these are still the things that bear evidence to the spark of divinity in each of us. The things that give us, our families, our communities, and our nation their own glimmer of greatness.

*Soli Deo Gloria*
John Perry
Nashville, Tennessee
Washington's Birthday, 2010

# ONE

# An American Citizen

JEB STUART'S ARRIVAL was a pleasant surprise for Colonel Robert E. Lee, U.S. Army. Lee was a man of action, more comfortable riding a frontier reconnaissance patrol than shuffling papers, and the chore of filling out a fire insurance application was one he surely enjoyed having interrupted. Lee had known Lieutenant Stuart since his plebe days at West Point seven years earlier when the colonel was commandant there. Usually neither of them would be in the plantation office of the Lee family home on this damp, chilly October morning. Lee's regular cavalry command was in Texas, and Stuart served in Kansas. The lieutenant was visiting Washington to discuss the patented belt attachment for a cavalry sword that he'd sold to the government. Across the

Potomac from the capital, Colonel Lee labored at his desk out of a sense of family duty.

Lee had never owned a house in his life, but he'd had a crash course in household financial management since the death of his father-in-law, George Washington Parke Custis. It was not just any house in his care. This was Arlington, one of the most famous plantations in Virginia, built and owned by the foster son of George Washington, and it was filled with elegant furniture and historic artifacts from Mount Vernon. The estate included 1,100 acres of land, fish hatcheries, vast stands of timber, a sawmill, and nearly two hundred slaves. When Mr. Custis died a widower, he left everything to his only surviving child, Mary, who was Colonel Lee's wife. Grand as the place was, it rested on shaky financial underpinnings. Mr. Custis had a taste for the finest in everything but no head for business. The estate accounts hadn't been balanced in nine years. When he died, no one knew how much money he had or how much he owed. Robert had taken leave from his military command for nearly two years to unscramble the books at Arlington in order to preserve its legacy for his wife and their seven children.

As an experienced senior officer with no day-to-day military responsibilities for the moment, Colonel Lee was tapped occasionally for courts-martial and other temporary duty in and around Washington. Lieutenant Stuart might have come to call that dank Monday morning with another routine assignment, but this matter was far more consequential. Reading the note Jeb handed him, the gracious and hospitable colonel didn't even take time to offer his young friend refreshment and a few minutes' conversation. He said a hasty good-bye to his wife and, still in civilian clothes, rode immediately with Stuart back to Washington. He'd been ordered by Secretary of War John Floyd to report to the War Department at once.

The night before, October 16, 1859, the army arsenal at Harpers Ferry, Virginia, had been raided and overrun by fanatic followers of a fire-breathing abolitionist named John Brown. Invaders poured into the unguarded facility and quickly disarmed the few soldiers on duty. By the next day, townspeople and the local militia had surrounded Brown and his men, but the abolitionists were barricaded in the firehouse and heavily armed. They'd also taken hostages, including Lewis Washington, the elderly great-grand-nephew of the first president. A company of soldiers from nearby Fort Monroe and marines from Washington were ordered to help the local defenders take back the arsenal, rescue the hostages, and capture the raiders. By Secretary Floyd's reckoning, Colonel Lee was the best available officer to lead this combined force.

John Brown, who also called himself Ossawattamie Brown, got his financial support from abolitionists in Kansas and the New England states. Three years earlier in a raid on Pottawatomie Creek, Kansas, his followers hacked five proslavery citizens to death with swords. He claimed the killings were God's will. After further organizing in Canada, Brown arrived in Harpers Ferry to steal its military weapons and ammunition. His grand plan was to lead a slave revolt and set up an independent homeland for liberated blacks in the Appalachian Mountains. The first step was to round up and arm volunteer guerrillas. Harpers Ferry was a logical place to go for weapons because besides housing the federal arsenal, it was home to a long list of gun and ammunition manufacturers.

Lee and Stuart arrived by train at Sandy Hook, a mile from Harpers Ferry, at ten o'clock that night to meet his command and plan a counterassault. To reduce the risk of shooting a hostage, they waited until daylight to send Stuart to the firehouse door with a white flag. The lieutenant carried a note demanding Brown and his men surrender and promising them safe treatment. Lee was afraid that once Brown read the note, he and his mob might try to fight their way out, kill the hostages, or both. Lee told Stuart not to negotiate. As soon as Brown turned down the offer, Stuart was to give a signal and Lee's troops would storm the firehouse with a dozen marines leading the way. Lewis Washington was more concerned about stopping Brown than he was about saving his own skin. "Never mind us," he yelled from inside. "Fire!"

Standing at the open firehouse door, Brown considered the ultimatum and then insisted on making a counterproposal. With that, Stuart waved his hat, Lee's units moved forward, and in less than five minutes the scuffle was over. John Brown was wounded by a sword and captured. Five of Brown's men died, but all thirteen hostages escaped unhurt. Lee sent the survivors under guard to Charleston, the county seat, for trial and filed his report, calling the incident a minor matter. He described Brown and his followers as "rioters" and Brown himself as "a fanatic madman."

Brown was convicted of high treason and murder and sentenced to hang. Northern abolitionists immediately anointed him "Saint John" and "Saint Just," claiming that "John Brown has twice as much right to hang Governor Wise [of Virginia] as Governor Wise has to hang him." The governor feared there might be riots in Harpers Ferry on December 2, the day that Brown was to be executed in Charleston, and he petitioned the federal government for protection. Lee returned to Harpers Ferry commanding more than three thousand marines and state militiamen, determined to keep the peace by a show of force. The rumors turned out to be false, and the armed rabble-rousers never showed. After Brown was hanged at 11:30 that morning, there was really nothing for the soldiers to do. Lee drilled the men in target practice to keep them occupied until they left town on December 12.

Lee finally got the paperwork at Arlington under control and, on February 10, 1860, headed for San Antonio to lead the Department of Texas. It was frankly a boring assignment, even if it was a departmental command. He missed his family, missed his beloved Virginia, and may well have wondered what the future held in store. Robert Edward Lee had been a commissioned officer in the U.S. Army for thirty-one years by then, twenty-three of them as a captain of engineers. At long last he'd been promoted to lieutenant colonel, but the chance for further advancement seemed slim. Three lieutenant colonels and nineteen colonels were ahead of him in line for a general's star. How long could he wait? Perhaps it was time to resign his commission and turn to managing Arlington, taking care of his disabled, arthritic wife, and spending time with the children who grew up while he was away on military assignment for years on end.

The election of Abraham Lincoln later that year put an end to whatever hope Lee had of living the life of a country squire. South Carolina, loudly unhappy for decades with the federal government's position on states' rights, had threatened to secede from the Union if Lincoln was elected. Two Democrats—Vice President

John C. Breckinridge and Senator Stephen Douglas of Illinois—ran in the national election, along with the Constitutional Union Party candidate, John Bell. In this four-way contest, Lincoln carried the new Republican Party to its first nationwide victory. Four days later South Carolina called for a convention to consider secession, and on December 20 the state declared itself separated from the United States. Texas started rumbling about seceding as well.

On January 23, 1861, Colonel Lee wrote a long letter to his son Custis, musing on the widening rift between North and South:

> As an American citizen, I take great pride in my country, her prosperity and institutions, and would defend any State if her rights were invaded. But I can anticipate no greater calamity for the country than a dissolution of the Union. It would be an accumulation of all the evils we complain of, and I am willing to sacrifice everything but honor for its preservation. . . . Secession is nothing but revolution. . . . Still, a Union that can only be maintained by swords and bayonets, and in which strife and civil war are to take the place of brotherly love and kindness, has no charm for me. . . . If the Union is dissolved and the government disrupted, I shall return to my native State and share the miseries of my people, and, save in defense, will draw my sword on no one.

The night before, he had shared the same thought with his dear Markie—Martha Custis Williams, a cousin by marriage and a favorite correspondent: "There is no sacrifice I am not ready to make for the preservation of the Union save that of honour. . . .

I wish for no other flag than the 'Star spangled banner' and no other air than 'Hail Columbia.' I still hope that the wisdom and patriotism of the nation will yet save it."

On February 1, 1861, Texas seceded from the Union and four days later joined the Confederate States of America, a growing list of disaffected states that claimed a constitutional right to form a new sovereign nation. Texas was the seventh member of the group, which since South Carolina seceded the previous December had already added Mississippi, Florida, Alabama, Georgia, and Louisiana. The day Texas joined, Virginia, to Lee's relief, voted to stay with the Union. But suddenly, Colonel Lee and the Department of Texas were U.S. soldiers on alien land. On February 19, Lee's superior, General David Emanuel Twiggs, surrendered his command to Confederate representatives in San Antonio and left the state. Twigg's headquarters forwarded an order to Lee to report in person to General in Chief Winfield Scott in Washington. Lee arrived home on March 1, four days before Lincoln was inaugurated, and within days the new president signed Lee's commission as a full colonel.

By then he had already been offered a commission as a general in the Confederate army. Though there is no record of Lee's reply to the Confederates, historian Douglas Southall Freeman suggests, "It is probable that he ignored the offer. He owed allegiance to only two governments, that of Virginia and that of the United States." And allegiance to one would soon mean fighting against the other.

The Lees had been in Virginia since 1641, four generations before the American Revolution. Not only had Colonel Lee's father-in-law grown up in George Washington's household, but Lee's father had fought beside Washington as a hero during the War of Independence. The Lees had been wed head, hand, and heart to Virginia for two centuries and to the United States as long as it had existed. Robert reflected a historic legacy: a career army officer, loyal and brave; a soldier and citizen who placed his duty above everything else. He was descended from generals, governors, crusaders, and royal counselors, born in the same room as two cousins who signed the Declaration of Independence.

Yet now, to uphold the honor of his convictions, Colonel Robert E. Lee would have to surrender his allegiance to the same nation that the Declaration announced and justified to the world. The nation Lee had served and defended all his life.

# TWO

## Light Horse Legacy

T HE  L EES  WERE  originally a Norman family. One of the first notable soldiers in the line was Launcelot de Léga, who invaded England with William the Conqueror at the Battle of Hastings in 1066. His descendant Lionel de Lee rode with Richard the Lionheart on the Third Crusade in 1191. Beginning ten years later, a line of nine Lees served as sheriffs of Shropshire into the seventeenth century. The family likely had an estate in Essex called Strafford Langton or Stratford Langton.

The first Lee in the New World was Richard Lee. Before crossing the Atlantic, he already knew the colonies as well as any Englishman. He served as secretary of the colony of Virginia and a member of the king's Privy Council, which managed the colony's affairs. Within a year after his arrival in 1641 he and his wife, Anne, received a thousand-acre plantation in York County that Lee named Paradise. He brought indentured servants with him, eventually releasing them from their obligations and giving them land. He then returned to England for another group of adventurers. An acquaintance described Richard Lee as "a man of good Stature, comely visage and generous nature." In time his holdings included stores, warehouses, ocean-going trade ships, and agricultural land.

A faithful royalist, Lee kept a low profile after King Charles I was executed and Oliver Cromwell took the reins of power four years later in 1653. Lee befriended the king's son in exile, offering support in exchange for a new royal commission should Charles II ever ascend the throne. When Cromwell died and the monarchy was restored, Lee became a great favorite at court. He returned to London from the New World almost every year, and brought back indentured servants who became free settlers. By 1659, his tobacco crop alone was worth £2,000 annually, roughly equivalent to $400,000 today. At his death in 1664 he owned 20,000 acres of land, half a dozen homes, and a fortune in ships, crops, and livestock.

He also owned chattel slaves. Tobacco, introduced to England by Virginia traders, had become hugely popular and profitable. It was a very labor-intensive crop, requiring work for which the average indentured servant had neither the stamina nor the inclination. Seeing how West Indian planters had thrived using African slaves, Americans soon followed suit. In 1625 there were twenty-five African slaves in Virginia; by 1671 there were two thousand.

In keeping with the English tradition of primogeniture, Richard Lee left most of his riches to his oldest son, John. When

John died a bachelor, the family fortune passed to the second son, Richard, who served in the Virginia House of Burgesses, the first deliberative body in America.

Young Richard found his life in danger during Bacon's Rebellion in 1676 when Nathaniel Bacon, a wealthy planter, led a revolt against the colonial governor. Governor William Berkeley refused to escalate a long-simmering conflict with the Indians that had grown into a series of bloody skirmishes with deaths on both sides. Furious at Berkeley's inaction, Bacon gathered a posse and demanded a commission to attack the Indians from the burgesses—including Lee—at gunpoint. The rebellion ended after Bacon died from dysentery a few months later, though by then he had burned the capital at Jamestown, including the governor's house, and held Lee captive for seven weeks.

When Richard died at his Mount Pleasant Plantation in 1714, he left a daughter and five sons, the fifth of which, Henry, was born in 1691. Henry's third and youngest son, also Henry, was born in 1729 and followed his grandfather into the Virginia House of Burgesses. Young Henry's next oldest brother, Thomas, became the first native-born governor of Virginia, and in the 1730s he built an imposing, austere-looking mansion in Westmoreland County that he named Stratford after the ancestral family home in Essex. Of Thomas's children, the eldest, Philip Ludwell Lee, would one day inherit Stratford, and the next two, Richard Henry and Francis Lightfoot, would become the only brothers to sign the Declaration of Independence.

Henry meanwhile settled his family at Leesylvania Plantation where his first son, the third Henry, was born in 1756, one of

173,000 white residents in Virginia that year alongside 120,000 blacks, almost all of them slaves. The growth of the institution of slavery and of the black population concerned the House of Burgesses, which described it in a petition to the king as "a trade of great inhumanity" that should be stopped. But even as they asked George III to permit colonial laws forbidding the slave trade, they admitted that "some of your Majesty's subjects may reap emoluments from this sort of traffic." With ever-increasing acreage devoted to tobacco, indigo, and cotton—all high-labor cash crops—slaves were a huge business. Outside of England, the biggest volume was controlled by Northern traders through their operations in Boston, Massachusetts, and Bristol, Rhode Island. These men had no interest in seeing their healthy profits disappear.

As the American colonies gained economic strength and political confidence, their chafing against British rule grew more open and strident. The third Henry Lee graduated from the College of New Jersey (later Princeton) in 1773, expecting to study law in England. Those plans changed three years later when America declared itself independent from Great Britain, Virginia prepared for war, and Governor Patrick Henry offered Lee, age twenty, a commission as a captain of cavalry. Henry Lee was a natural leader, energetic, resourceful, and fearless. In two years he was promoted to major, commanding a combined force of cavalry and infantry known as Lee's Legion. On August 19, 1779, Major Lee led an attack on a British-occupied fort at Paulus Hook, New Jersey (present-day Jersey City). Finding sick soldiers, women, and children inside, he didn't burn the barracks as planned, but took 159 soldiers prisoner.

Reporting the victory in a letter to Congress, General George Washington wrote, "The Major displayed a remarkable degree of prudence, address and bravery upon this occasion, which does the highest honor to himself and all the officers and men under his command. The situation of the fort rendered the attempt critical and the success brilliant."

Lee was awarded a specially struck gold medal—the only officer below the rank of general to be so honored—and $15,000 to distribute among his troops. Admirers called him "Light Horse Harry," the dashing, capable, and accomplished young leader of light horse cavalry. Lee became a delegate to the Continental Congress and, still in his thirties, served three one-year terms as governor of Virginia beginning in 1791. President Washington quietly supported him for the office, and their friendship, both personal and professional, continued through Washington's two terms as president.

In 1794, Lee helped Washington lead federal troops against the Whiskey Rebellion in Pennsylvania, one of the earliest tests of the nation's new federal powers. After the government put a tax on whiskey to help pay its war debts, Pennsylvanians who thought the tax was unlawful refused to pay it. Lee, Washington, and Alexander Hamilton led more than twelve thousand troops against the uprising. In the face of such force, the rebellion evaporated.

Light Horse Harry, became a member of the U.S. House of Representatives in 1799. There he wrote the famous words spoken by John Marshall at Washington's funeral: the first president was also "first in war, first in peace, and first in the hearts of his countrymen."

The forty-five-year-old Lee retired from public life in 1801.

He was a man of honor and accomplishment, one who had led magnificently and served faithfully. His lineage was noble, his property substantial. Yet this publicly successful man had struggled for years in his private life, and all too soon his brilliance would be eclipsed by disappointment and tragedy.

In 1782 Henry had married his second cousin Matilda Ludwell Lee, known as "the divine Matilda," daughter of the late Philip Ludwell Lee and granddaughter of Henry's Uncle Thomas. General Washington may have contributed wine for the wedding supper. The couple lived on a grand scale at Stratford with Matilda's mother and her second husband, Philip Richard Fendall. But the peace and financial security of the household were threatened by Henry's weakness for land speculation. Always thinking the next scheme would yield a fortune, he went deeper into debt as the years passed.

At Matilda's death in 1790, she left three young children. Three years later, while he was governor of Virginia, Harry married Anne Hill Carter, daughter of Charles Carter, descendant of King Robert II of Scotland and master of Shirley Plantation, one of the largest and wealthiest plantations in Virginia (still today a working farm and home to the eleventh generation of the family). The French had offered Lee a commission as a major general to fight in their Revolution. Carter was wary of Lee's cavalier inclinations and gave his consent on the condition that Lee give up any notion of fighting in France. After Lee decided to stay home, Washington sent a warm note of congratulation: "As we are told that you have exchanged the rugged and dangerous fields of Mars for the soft and pleasurable bed of Venus, I do in this, as I shall in everything you may pursue like unto it, good and laudable, wish you all imaginable success and happiness."

Carter, concerned for his daughter's own "success and happiness," set up a trust for her that Harry could never touch because Carter feared that Harry would lose the funds in bad business ventures, just as he had lost his own money.

Carter's concern was well founded. Among other investments gone sour was a deal to finance a speculative land purchase that cost Lee $40,000 (more than $700,000 today). Every attempt to recover his losses only made matters worse. After their marriage, Anne moved to Stratford. Of their five children who survived, three were born by the time Matilda's stepfather died in 1805. Like Charles Carter, Philip Fendall feared that if Henry could get his hands on the family fortune, he would squander it. To prevent that, he left Stratford to Matilda and Harry's only surviving son, Henry, to be held in trust by Anne until her stepson turned twenty-one. She would have a home and some income from the estate at least until then.

By 1806, Anne was expecting again. When her father died that fall, she made a very uncomfortable trip to Shirley to be with her extended family. By Christmas, she was back at Stratford, sick, saddened, and worried about her husband's debts. Even her carriage had been sold to try and keep up with the relentless claims. Her house and property were shielded from the collectors, but she constantly had to scrape for cash to meet routine household expenses. Once her father's estate was settled, she received enough direct income from that source to cover the basics for herself and her children, but nothing more.

On January 19, 1807, Anne Carter Lee gave birth to a healthy son in the large corner bedroom on the main floor at Stratford, where so many Lees before him had been born. She named him Robert Edward, after two of her brothers. Scarcely two years later, in April 1809, Light Horse Harry was hauled off to debtors' prison for a year. Before then Robert's half brother, Henry, had come of age and inherited the family estate. Perhaps Harry didn't want to be a houseguest of his own son. Whatever the reason, after his release from prison, Harry moved Anne and their children to a modest townhouse on Cameron Street in Alexandria. A year or so later, the family settled into a fine home on Oronoco Street that belonged to a distant relative, William Fitzhugh, whose great-grandmother was a granddaughter of the immigrant Richard Lee. Later they also lived a while on Washington Street.

George Washington's name and memory were still very much alive in Alexandria then, only ten years after his death. Even as a small boy, Robert must have been aware of it. When he went to church, the preacher read aloud from Washington's personal Bible. When he walked the streets of the town, he saw the post office and Masonic temple where Washington had often visited. These experiences built upon the Washington legend that Robert already knew from hearing of his father's wartime adventures.

Robert may have also sensed that life was far more difficult than it had been in those heroic times. His father, the former war hero and governor, had been in prison while his mother struggled to meet the family's expenses. During his first few impressionable years, Robert lived in four different homes. Then came a family crisis that overshadowed everything else. In the summer of 1812 a string of long-festering disputes between the United States and Great Britain erupted into war. Harry Lee believed that America should not be drawn into another conflict. When President James Madison called for a declaration of war, the *Federal Republican* newspaper came out against the president. Within days a mob destroyed the newspaper's presses and burned its building. Lee helped the paper restart operations in a new location, which was attacked and ruined on July 27 by a crowd so violent that Lee was taken into protective custody.

Instead of cooling off, the mob rioted, breaking into the jail and beating Lee senseless. They knifed him repeatedly, tried to cut off his nose, and left him for dead in a pile of bodies. Miraculously, he survived. Eleven days after the attack, Lee's doctor reported, "He cannot yet converse or take any other substance except liquids, and of these very little. He is restored to the use of his mental powers and is able to make himself understood by uttering a word or two at a time."

Henry Lee never recovered from his beating. His nose was permanently disfigured, and he had trouble speaking and walking for the rest of his life. In 1813, without explanation, he left his family in their borrowed lodgings and sailed for Barbados. It may have been a desperate attempt to escape his creditors. Or perhaps he thought he would improve his broken health or find the fortune that had eluded him elsewhere.

Robert was six then, scarcely old enough to remember his father well or to have spent much time with him. What must the boy have thought at that age, saying good-bye to a figure who was something of a stranger yet connected with him as only a father and a son can be? As Robert learned to read, he pored over letters his father sent home asking about the family, especially Anne's oldest son, Charles Carter. After Charles came Anne Kinloch, Sydney Smith, Robert, and last of all, Catherine Mildred, who was born after the family moved to Alexandria. In one typical letter to his wife Harry wrote, "Robert was always good, and will be confirmed in his happy turn of mind by his ever-watchful and affectionate mother."

A year after his father left, Robert weathered the British invasion of Alexandria during the war that Harry Lee had argued so passionately against. On August 28, 1814, the British sailed up the Potomac and occupied the town, demanding a large tribute. Having watched the invaders torch the U.S. Capitol four days before, the mayor acquiesced. We have no record of where Robert was or what he saw then, but it's likely that he went to visit relatives in the country, far from the fires and bloodshed.

Even in peacetime, Robert never had the luxury of a settled home and family life. He was raised by a single mother who moved her children from one place to another as circumstances required. His notion of family came not from parents and siblings, but from the tribe of Lees, Carters, Fitzhughs, Randolphs, and other interrelated clans that spent all year visiting each other and sending their children back and forth. King Carter had had twelve children and passed down the tendency to sire big families. Robert's grandfather Charles, one of King Carter's grandchildren, had twenty-three children of his own.

Robert gained a sense of belonging by mixing with this happy crowd of cousins and kinfolk, especially during long visits to his mother's relatives at Shirley and to William Fitzhugh's equally magnificent plantation, Ravensworth, on 22,000 acres in Fairfax County. The Carter family was so large that Charles Carter ran schools for the clan, one for girls at Shirley and another for boys at Eastern View Plantation in Fauquier County. This school allowed Robert to keep up with his studies during his travels. On a trip home to Alexandria, Robert seemed a little headstrong to his mother, but her sister Mrs. Randolph didn't think so. She called Robert "a most engaging child" and declared he was easy to handle. However, if Robert ever did become a problem, her advice to his mother was to do what she did to her own boys: "Whip and pray, and pray and whip."

A whipping was unlikely. Whenever his relations mentioned Robert in their letters, they invariably wrote about what a good boy he was, how obedient and self-assured beyond his years he seemed. Traveling so much, Robert learned early on to be comfortable as a guest, accepting hospitality graciously and being at ease in other people's homes. He grew up sharing bedrooms and dining tables with a constantly changing cluster of cousins—playing, riding, swimming, and exploring the woods with whoever was there to enjoy them with him. Along the way he became completely at ease in crowds, and he mastered the art of polite conversation in any situation. Even so, he seemed more relaxed with friends and family than with strangers. This characteristic made him appear aloof in later years, but it was really shyness. It just took him a while to warm up sometimes.

Soon after Robert's brother Charles left for Harvard in 1816, their father sent word that he was coming home. His reasons for returning were as much a mystery as his reasons for leaving. He may have felt strong enough to meet his creditors and clear the cloud of debt that tormented him; it could have been that he knew the end was near, and he wanted to see his family once more. In those days there was no regular passenger traffic on the ocean. Voyagers had to find transportation where they could. In time Harry caught a ship heading for Savannah, with plans to sail from there to Virginia. He became gravely ill on the way and came ashore at Dungeness, Cumberland Island, Georgia, on property owned by the daughter of his former commander Nathanael Greene. Lee died there on March 25, 1818, though his family didn't learn the details until the fall.

Robert had already taken on household chores for his mother out of necessity. With no father present in the family, the sons had to tackle day-to-day responsibilities as best they could. Within two years of their father's death, Robert's brother Carter was practicing law in Washington, and his brother Smith had gone to sea. That left a thirteen-year-old boy to take care of a mother who was declining in health, an older sister who was chronically sick, and a younger sister who was only nine.

It was a life of hard work and great responsibility that Robert accepted without complaint. For reasons Robert might never understand, his father had failed his family. Robert would not.

# THREE

# Making of a Gentleman

R OBERT ' S ADOLESCENCE REVOLVED around making family visits to Ravensworth and Shirley, caring for his mother, and getting an education. Beginning around 1820, he attended a private academy in Alexandria where he was an excellent student. His sister Anne spent time away from home receiving medical attention, and she later married, leaving Robert, sister Mildred, and their mother alone in the Alexandria townhouse. This living arrangement may help explain why all his life Robert especially enjoyed the company of women and girls.

As a boy, he acquired the habits of responsibility, punctuality, courtesy, and attention to detail. His mother's health and comfort became a central focus of his life. By his midteens, Robert evidently did the shopping, kept household accounts, and generally served as head of the family. He even carried his mother in his arms to and from her carriage on days she was too weak to walk.

Almost as soon as his relatives started noticing Robert's manners, they also commented on his handsome features. Teenage Robert had thick black hair and eyebrows, a chiseled jaw, and lively, piercing dark brown eyes. His high forehead, elegant profile, and full, sensual lips were cast in the mold of his father's, but more trim and proportional. Early on he became notorious (in a good way) for clever teasing and ribbing, but never made someone the butt of an embarrassing joke. He was a sly, irrepressible flirt who never offended. Then and later, observers commented on his mix of warmth and decorum.

The boy grew into a man tall for his generation at just under six feet. He was an expert rider who loved nothing more than spending time on horseback, which helped develop the tapered silhouette and powerful limbs that formed what one British journalist later said was the handsomest man he ever saw. He carried himself magnificently, shoulders square, chin up, lithe and graceful in the saddle and on foot.

Yet for all his presence and refinement, the adolescent Lee never seemed haughty or prideful. The humility that so marked his life formed early as well. He never considered himself superior to others.

Robert had no inherited wealth or position, no plantation, and no money for college. Highborn sons of modest means could choose from only a few socially acceptable careers. This son of a governor had no interest in politics or the law, no taste for oratory or the public spotlight. Other than rote family prayers and religious conventions of the Episcopal church they regularly attended, he wasn't drawn to the ministry or theology. The time he spent caring for his mother convinced him he wasn't suited to be a doctor.

Another possibility was a military commission. Around the time he finished at the Alexandria academy in 1823, Robert decided to apply for an appointment to the military academy at West Point, New York. Founded by the Corps of Engineers in 1802, the academy was a prestige assignment and—particularly good news for Robert—it was free. Applicants were selected by the president of the United States upon recommendation of the secretary of war, and competition for the limited number of slots was intense.

Robert's mother decided to appeal directly to the secretary, John C. Calhoun, but needed a letter of introduction and recommendation. William Fitzhugh, their relative and landlord, gladly sent a letter to Secretary Calhoun that Robert delivered in person. The secretary received other letters on Robert's behalf, including one signed by seven members of Congress. Many of them were from people who didn't know the boy personally and so emphasized his father's reputation as a war hero and friend of President Washington. On March 11, 1824, Robert Edward Lee was officially accepted at West Point, though he had to wait until the next academic year because there were so many new students.

Eager to improve himself and make the most of his time, Robert spent that year and a half tutoring with a Quaker named James Hallowell who opened an academy in the house next door to the Lees. Hallowell later remembered Lee as "a most exemplary pupil in every respect. He was never behind time in his studies; never failed in a single recitation; was perfectly observant of the rules and regulations of the institution; was gentlemanly, unobtrusive, and respectful in all his deportment to teacher and his fellow students."

The day before Hallowell moved in, October 14, 1824, was one of the most exciting in Robert's young life. President James Monroe had invited the Marquis de Lafayette to make a valedictory tour of the United States, and that was the day he visited the Lees. Lafayette, then sixty-seven, was a wealthy French aristocrat who had fought with honor under Washington's command and was wounded at Brandywine. Along with visits to Mount Vernon and to former President Thomas Jefferson, still the master of Monticello at eighty-one, the marquis wanted especially to call on the widow of his friend Henry Lee. He spent part of the day with her and the family at their house on Oronoco Street. Doubtless it was a bittersweet experience for Robert, having distant memories of his father reawakened by the presence of one who had known him well and remembered him with fond admiration.

Three days later, on October 17, Lafayette arrived at Mount Vernon. His host there shared Robert's fascination with Washington. George Washington Parke Custis was the grandson of Martha Washington by her first marriage to Daniel Parke Custis. After his father, John Parke Custis, died in 1781, he and his sister, Eleanor, were adopted by the general. The two children grew up at Mount Vernon, and Custis came to consider himself the keeper of Washington's legacy. He designed his own plantation nearby, Arlington, as a living memorial to his foster grandfather. After Martha died in 1802, Custis spent lavishly to acquire Washington family belongings he didn't already have, including uniforms, silver, and the general's red canvas campaign tent.

Mr. Custis was related by marriage to Robert's mother. His wife, Mary Fitzhugh, was the sister of William Fitzhugh and a granddaughter of Charles Carter of Shirley Plantation; Anne Carter Lee was one of Charles Carter's great-grandchildren.

Custis had tagged along on Lafayette's last visit to Mount Vernon in 1783 as a three-year-old toddler holding tightly to one of his grandfather's thick fingers. During this second visit, Mr. Custis presented Lafayette with a lock of Washington's hair, his umbrella, and a cup and saucer from the Washington state china. He also rode in a parade with the French dignitary and his son: George Washington Parke Custis and Georges Washington de Lafayette sitting side by side in the coach.

Robert was there too, as a parade marshal. During the festivities, he caught the eye of a childhood friend he'd seen many times at Ravensworth and also on visits to Arlington. Of George and Mary Custis's four children, only one had survived infancy. Mary Anna Randolph Custis was a year younger than Robert and, like him, had grown up hearing about the famous first president. As a girl, she played among the Mount Vernon furniture and household items stored in the unfinished ballroom at Arlington.

Mary was personable and popular, and loved the frequent visits she and her mother made to plantations of various cousins and friends. Eager to stimulate her daughter's intellect, Mrs. Custis sometimes took Mary to the visitors' gallery of the Supreme Court to hear cases being argued. One day a visitor from out of town noticed her "placid and winning face" and mentioned her in his journal: "She was richly but plainly attired, as was her mother, and there was a modest and reserved dignity about both of them that significantly bespoke their rank and bringing up. Miss Custis was described to me by those who knew her best as a young lady of sound and vigorous intellect, in which judgment and discrimination decidedly predominated."

Within a year after Lafayette's visit, Miss Custis received a marriage proposal from a congressman named Sam Houston, later governor of Tennessee, president of the Republic of Texas, and a U.S. senator. Thirty-two, successful, ambitious, and a friend of Andrew Jackson, he courted Mary even though she was only half his age. Houston visited Arlington several times, dined with the family, and wrote Mary poetry. But in the end she rejected the congressman's attentions. It may be that she already had her eye on her cousin Robert.

In June 1825, Robert left Virginia for New York, arriving months early for school to become familiar with the routine and the long list of rules that defined a cadet's life. Cadets were not permitted to drink alcohol, play cards, use tobacco, or read novels. Visiting hours were strictly limited, and students could not leave the campus without special permission. Regimented as life was, Robert adapted to it quickly. He already had such self-discipline that he took the military discipline in stride.

His first year at the academy, Robert was honored as a Distinguished Cadet, one of the top five in the class, with special proficiency in mathematics and French. He was also named staff sergeant for his upcoming second year, the highest honor a freshman could earn. During his sophomore, or "third class," year, he spent more time reading on his own, including a new edition of his father's *Memoirs of the War in the Southern Department* edited by his half brother Henry. Lee also became an acting assistant professor of mathematics, mostly a job tutoring struggling freshmen, but it paid ten dollars a month on top of his regular stipend.

In the summer of 1827 he saw his mother for the first time in two years and was shocked at how frail she was. She probably had narcolepsy and was terrified of being buried alive. She also had an advanced, painful case of tuberculosis. To her older son, Smith, she wrote, "My disease is an unconquerable one, but the symptoms at present do not threaten a speedy death."

On a brighter note, Lee took a trip that summer to Kinloch Plantation in Fauquier County, home of his distant cousin Edward Carter Turner. With only one vacation allowed from the academy in four years, it's noteworthy that Lee chose to visit Kinloch because Mary Custis would be there. Robert arrived in his cadet uniform, a trim gray coat with metal buttons and gold braid, white cotton duck trousers, and a seven-inch black leather hat topped with a pompon. He was twenty, a mature man, a soldier strengthened and developed by discipline and training. As in the past, friends noted his "manly beauty," flawless posture, thick dark hair, and classically handsome face. Some at West Point called him the Marble Model. It may have been on this visit that Robert and Mary Custis realized they were in love.

Immersing himself in his third year at the academy, Lee continued his math tutoring while studying drawing—two hours a day including landscape, topography, and the human figure—plus chemistry, physics, and military drill. The fourth and final year concentrated more on engineering skills. Robert finished West Point without getting a single demerit. Although he ranked second in his class, he was appointed adjutant of the corps, the highest honor bestowed by the academy. As a top graduate, Lee got to choose his preferred branch of service, and he picked the Corps of Engineers.

Describing him in those years, fellow Virginian and classmate Joseph E. Johnston wrote,

> No other youth or man so united the qualities that win warm friendship and command high respect. For he was full of sympathy and kindness, genial and fond of gay conversation, even fun, while his correctness of demeanor and attention to all duties, personal and official, and a dignity as much a part of himself as the elegance of his person, gave him a superiority that everyone acknowledged in his heart.

A freshman from the year that Lee was corps adjutant remembered, "All his accomplishments and alluring virtues appeared natural to him, and he was free from the anxiety, distrust and awkwardness that attend a sense of inferiority." At a later time another admirer would call him "the most *entire* gentleman I ever saw."

As Robert entered his last year at the Academy, his mother became weaker and more helpless. By the time he graduated she was too sick to live on her own. With daughter Anne married and Mildred engaged, Mrs. Lee moved in with her son Carter for a while, then settled in at Ravensworth where her uncle William Fitzhugh and his wife, Maria, could take care of her. Robert rushed back from West Point immediately after his July 1 commissioning ceremony to be with her at the end. During her last days, he scarcely left her room, and when she died on July 10, 1829, he was standing faithfully beside her bed. Reporting her passing, the *National Intelligencer* stated, "Her death is such as might have been expected from her in life—exhibiting the resignation and composure of a practical Christian, conscious of having faithfully discharged her duties to God and her fellow creatures."

Robert literally had no place to call home after his mother's death because his first posting as a lieutenant did not begin immediately. On August 11 he was ordered to report by mid-November to Cockspur Island, a forlorn spot on the Georgia coast surrounded by marshland, where the government was building a fort. In the meantime he stayed with his brother in Georgetown and visited Ravensworth, Eastern View, and Arlington. He saw Mary Custis at all of these country places, and being with her lifted his spirits. Spending time with Mary and other friends and family brought out his natural lightheartedness. One of his cousins remembered him that summer "as full of life, fun and particularly of teasing, as any of us."

By the time he left for Georgia, Robert had gotten permission from Mr. and Mrs. Custis to write Mary from Cockspur Island. At first Mrs. Custis read his letters, as she read all of Mary's mail. It was a sign of her respect for him that, when she heard it made Robert uncomfortable, she passed his envelopes, unopened, to her daughter. Writing to tell her beau that his letters would be private from then on, she said her mother "promises not to require a sight of your letters, though I told her I could not imagine anything you had to say that she might not see, yet I know it is sometimes unpleasant, so you are perfectly at liberty to say what you please, trusting in your discretion to say only what is right."

## FOUR

# Dear Mary

COCKSPUR ISLAND, IN the Savannah River twelve miles downstream from the city of the same name, was practically at sea level, flooded daily by the tide and swamped in heavy weather. In summer the place was overrun with mosquitoes and a breeding ground for disease. Winter brought miserably cold water and frigid Atlantic wind. Arriving November 1, Robert spent days on end working up to his armpits in chilly, gelatinous mud.

One saving grace was that his friend and fellow officer Jack Mackay lived in Savannah, and his family welcomed Robert as one of their own. Though neither as large nor as old as the social aristocracy of Virginia, the leading families of Savannah enjoyed elegant and cultured lives. During the winter of 1829–30, Robert threw himself into the thick of the social season there while Mary

Custis went on her usual rounds of visits, and she received visitors and hosted parties at Arlington. Custis hospitality was legendary. Part of the plantation grounds along the Potomac was open to the public, furnished with a dance pavilion, and accessible from Washington via a small steam ferry, the *GWP Custis*. Though Robert and Mary enjoyed their separate worlds that winter, their commitment to each other never wavered.

Summer 1830 brought the usual heat, humidity, mosquitoes, and sand flies to Cockspur Island, halting work for the season. Robert took leave to visit his brother Carter, now living in New York, then sailed for Washington and Arlington to spend the rest of his vacation with his dear Mary.

Though Mary had long since given her heart to her cousin and childhood friend, one element of their relationship troubled her. She hadn't talked about it with anyone but him. Even her mother, her closest confidante, didn't know about the struggle in her daughter's heart over whether Robert was a Christian. Did he truly hold Christ in his heart? How could she know for sure? If he was not a Christian, could she become his wife with a clear conscience anyway? The question hadn't mattered so much before this summer. But writing in her prayer journal on July 10, Mary unburdened her heart:

> I feel no desires now for the vain pleasures of the world. I feel as if I could give them up from love to my God. But could I give up my attachment to him I love? I thought I [could] do even that, if my Heavenly Father had required it, but our hearts are so deceitful that I doubt my sincerity. I did *not feel*

that He required that sacrifice. Oh God search my heart . . .
if I am deceived by Satan open Thou my eyes. . . . Oh draw
him also to Thee that we may with one heart & one mind live
to the glory of our Redeemer. May he never draw my soul
from Thee.

Mary had begun her prayer journal only a week before, on
July 4, after a life-changing religious transformation. On May
21, 1830, William Henry Fitzhugh died at the age of thirty-eight
during a visit to Maryland. He left behind the vast Ravensworth
estate, another 1,200 acres at Chatham where he was born, and
the townhouse at 607 Oronoco Street in Alexandria where Robert
and his family once lived. Yet Maria, his childless widow, found
no pleasure in any of it or in any of the friends, family, and diver-
sions surrounding her. It seemed like nothing on earth could
relieve her agony. Seeing her aunt suffer so miserably made Mary
wonder whether there wasn't more to the world than relation-
ships and material wealth. Maybe there was a spiritual treasure,
eternal and ever present, that nothing on earth could take away.
Looking back, she confided in her journal on July 22:

> The view of [Aunt Maria's] utter wretchedness impressed me
> with the vanity of earthly things, and one night I prayed fer-
> vently that God would comfort her. I do not recollect whether
> I prayed for myself—I returned home still thirsting after the
> world & its honours.
>
> We went to Ravensworth where I had spent my happiest
> hours—there all was desolation and woe—there first I prayed

to my God to change my heart & make me His true & faithful servant until my life's end. I was led on by His blessed spirit from day to day more & more to desire His favour, to see my base ingratitude & unworthiness to Him who so loved us as to give His only son to die for us, to see my utter helplessness, to cast all my hopes upon my Saviour, to feel a willingness to give up all I had formerly delighted in for His sake & afterwards through His grace not to desire them, to feel my heart melted with love to God though sometimes it was hard enough.

On October 5, four days after her twenty-second birthday, Mary was confirmed at Christ Church in Alexandria. "I have communed today for the first time," she declared. "I expected it would be a rejoicing time, but I was bowed down with a spirit of infirmity, a sense of unworthiness & ingratitude & did not enjoy it as I expected. . . . Oh my Father, wilt Thou bless this ordinance to the refreshing & quickening of this dull soul! I know I was born again. That feeble as I am, I am called by grace to follow in my Saviour's footsteps."

Mary wrote at length in her journal that summer about her spiritual journey and her concern over Robert's soul. Nothing survives to explain Robert's view of the matter. It wasn't that Mary saw anything disturbing in his spiritual convictions. The problem was that she had no concrete evidence that Robert held Christ in his heart the way she did, that he too was "born again." We can imagine her, in all the passion and conviction of her new-found faith, pouring her heart out to cool, never-flustered Robert, who was open to the dialogue but couldn't find the subjective spiritual feelings inside his engineer's mind and heart to tell her what she wanted so desperately to hear.

Probably Robert stayed at Arlington until after Mary's confirmation, then went to visit his sister in Baltimore and back to Cockspur Island. Just after Lieutenant Lee left her, Mary became so gravely ill that she and her family thought she might not survive. On November 21, after the danger had passed, she reached once more for her journal:

> When laid in a bed of sickness I thought I may now die, this may be my last sickness. My heart could say sincerely, Lord, if it be Thy will, take Thy child to dwell with Thee, for it is far better to depart & be with Thee than to remain here. . . . I have often thought that the love & goodness of God has been so great & astonishing to me, that He designed me for an early tomb.

By then, Robert was back in the marsh to discover much of the work done before the heat of the summer was ruined in a gale. He immediately began working on repairs and had part of the embankment rebuilt by the time a new commanding officer was assigned to Cockspur. The officer did not take long to decide that the fort as planned was unsuitable for the site and new plans were required. In April, Robert was ordered to Hampton Roads, Virginia, to help finish construction of Fort Monroe there. The main part of the project was complete, and Lee's essential but mundane job was to figure expenses, order supplies, and supervise men excavating the remaining earthworks. His immediate superior, Captain Andrew Talcott, became a great friend, as did Mrs. Talcott, the former Harriet Randolph Hackley, a renowned beauty and a cousin of Mary Custis.

Whenever it was possible, Lieutenant Lee traveled back to Arlington to see Mary. Evenings after dinner they sat with Mr. and Mrs. Custis, discussing current events or listening to Mr. Custis play his violin. No doubt they talked of President Andrew Jackson, the Tennessee cotton planter and hero of the Battle of New Orleans, who had brought a whirlwind of change to Washington. And they likely spoke of Mr. Custis's interest in the American Colonization Society, established to free the slaves in America and repatriate them to the African nation of Liberia founded specifically for that purpose.

They all enjoyed the Waverly novels of Sir Walter Scott, which Mr. Custis and Robert took turns reading aloud. One day when Robert had been reading, Mrs. Custis suggested to Mary that he might like some refreshment. Mary walked from the sitting room to the Mount Vernon sideboard in the dining room and was cutting a piece of fruitcake when she felt an arm slip around her waist. It was Robert. He asked her to be his wife.

She'd made up her mind long ago: the answer was yes.

Mary's parents had seen the moment coming for a long time too. Mrs. Custis was elated and immediately gave her consent. Mr. Custis wasn't quite as eager. He had known Light Horse Harry and had delivered a stirring oration at the funeral of another officer who was murdered the night that Harry was beaten. He also knew about the Lee family's financial struggles. Custis had lived beyond his means all his life and would doubtless have preferred—from a purely business standpoint—a young man from one of the wealthy families in his circle of acquaintances.

Another factor would have been a recent blot on the Lee family name. Robert's half brother Henry had sold Stratford to satisfy his creditors and moved to the Hermitage, President Jackson's plantation outside Nashville, to work as an advisor and speechwriter. Jackson offered Henry the choice assignment as U.S. ambassador to Morocco, and Henry had already moved overseas when the Senate confirmation process began. During the proceedings, word got out that years earlier, Henry had had an affair with his young sister-in-law, who at the time was his legal ward. In February 1830, the senators voted unanimously against the appointment. Stranded across the Atlantic and suddenly unemployed, Henry went to Italy and finally settled in Paris, where he struggled to earn a living as a writer until his death in 1837.

Whatever misgivings Mr. Custis might have had, his daughter's wedding was set for Thursday, June 30, 1831, at Arlington. In the days leading up to the big event, the great house above the Potomac filled to bursting with guests. Some slept on cots, others three to a bed, generating an atmosphere not of inconvenience but of adventure and excitement.

As the hour approached for the wedding, a summer rainstorm soaked the lawn, driving the guests indoors from the carefully clipped gardens. The minister, Rev. Reuel Keith, head of the Virginia Theological Seminary in Alexandria, arrived on horseback drenched to the skin. Escorted upstairs to change, he found few dry clothing options available. Lee, as well as four of the six groomsmen, was in uniform, and the guests had few spare dress clothes. The only option was the wardrobe of Mr. Custis, who was considerably stouter and shorter than the reverend. Fortunately Keith's pastoral vestments were still dry and hid the ill-fitting outfit.

The ceremony that evening was in the parlor to the right of the grand entry foyer. Three arches separating that room from the dining room were hung with garlands from the estate and lighted by the porch light from Mount Vernon in the hall and by George Washington's candelabra on the table. Through the center arch, Mary could see the sideboard where she and Robert had stood when he proposed. When the piano music began, Mr. Custis escorted his daughter down the stairs and into the hall, between a double row of groomsmen and bridesmaids, to her place beside Robert under the center arch. Robert was in his summer dress uniform and sported long, luxuriant dark side whiskers nearly to his jaw.

The bride and groom joined hands; her hand trembled in his. Rev. Keith read the Episcopal service, Robert later recalled, "as if he had been reading my death warrant." Describing the occasion, one of the bridesmaids, Marietta Turner, wrote, "My cousin, always a modest and affectionate girl, was never lovelier. Though midsummer rain denied the company the enjoyment of the gardens, which commanded an unparalleled view of the Potomac and the city of Washington, the evening was one long to be remembered," due in part to "the elegance and simplicity of the bride's parents presiding over the feast and the happiness of the grinning servants."

In those days newlyweds didn't disappear right away on a honeymoon, but remained several days to visit with the out-of-town wedding guests. At last on July 5, the wedding couple and

Mrs. Custis went for a visit to Ravensworth, then on to other kin at Woodlawn and Kinloch Plantations. By early August, Lieutenant and Mrs. Robert E. Lee arrived at Old Point Comfort, near Fort Monroe, to set up housekeeping in Quarters No. 17, which they would share with Captain Talcott, and Talcott's sister and her family. From the world of Arlington, Stratford, Shirley, and Ravensworth, the Lees would be adjusting to their new home in two dirt-floored rooms.

Henry "Light Horse Harry" Lee, a captain of cavalry at 20, was a war hero, governor of Virginia, and a member of the U.S. House of Representatives. Sentenced to debtor's prison in 1809 and left for dead by a rioting mob in 1812, he abandoned his son Robert and the rest of his family to seek his fortune in Barbados.

Anne Hill Carter Lee was of a distinguished family descended from King Robert II of Scotland. She married "Light Horse Harry" when the widower was governor, enduring years of financial hardship because of his thirst for speculation.

Stratford Hall, the Lee ancestral home built c. 1730 by Thomas Lee, first native born governor of Virginia. Robert E. Lee was born here in 1807.

Lee portrait painted in Baltimore by William West, 1838. Lee's wife wanted him portrayed in his dress uniform; West painted the face while waiting for the clothes to arrive.

Mary Anna Custis Lee, painted at the same time as her husband. Though only 29, the strain of her serious illnesses is beginning to show through the refined features.

# FIVE

# A Duty Imposed

THE NEWLYWEDS ARRIVED at Old Point Comfort with furniture from Arlington and one household slave, Cassie, whom Mrs. Custis sent with them. Mr. Custis soon started shipping generous gifts of food—ham, bacon, molasses, vegetables, flour, and fish—by steamboat from his Romancoke and White House Plantations. Mary had never kept house before and never had to get along without a small army of servants, but she gamely tackled her new responsibilities. In his teasing way, Robert later wrote a friend that "Mrs. L. is somewhat addicted to laziness and forgetfulness in her housekeeping," but that "she does her best, or in her mother's words, 'The Spirit is willing but the flesh is weak.'" Unfortunately for Mary, these few words, taken out of context and misinterpreted as genuine criticism, have branded her in history as unkempt and incapable and her husband as a stern-faced critic. In fact, Lee was displaying his well-known tendency to be what later generations would call a kidder, and Mary, considering her life experience up to then, was doing as well in her new role as anyone had a right to expect.

The lieutenant and his bride were scarcely settled when the mayor of nearby Norfolk warned the post commander, Colonel Abram Eustis, of a slave uprising. A black man named Nat Turner believed God had told him to kill his "enemies" with their own weapons. Turner was convinced that a recent solar eclipse and other natural phenomena were God's signs that it was time to act. On the night of August 21, Turner and a few followers broke into one house at a time, freeing the slaves to join them and slaughtering the white families with knives, hatchets, and clubs. By the time they were stopped, they had killed about sixty white people, many of them children. At one house ten children were decapitated and their bodies piled on the front lawn.

Turner escaped, even though three companies from Fort Monroe and troops from two warships joined forces to stop the insurrection and catch its leaders. The revolt ended quickly, but as many as two hundred or more blacks were killed in retribution for the Turner murders. Two months later Nat Turner was captured. He was found guilty of murder on November 5 and hanged on November 11. After he died on the gallows, his body was decapitated, skinned, and quartered.

Afraid that more slaves would follow Turner's example, Colonel Eustis issued a stern order: "No negroes or persons of color of either sex, other than the servants of officers, and those employed in the Hospital and Quarter Masters Dept. are to be harboured or tolerated within the walls of the Fort." Lee protested this decision both to his commander and to his superiors in Washington. He thought it was unnecessary and also impractical because the engineering work crews were black and needed to go in and out of the fort all day for drinking water and mortar. Also the draftsmen expected their slaves to be able to come and go at will. But the colonel's order stood.

Robert and Mary believed in gradual emancipation. Mr. Custis still belonged to the American Colonization Society, whose members included President James Monroe and Supreme Court Chief Justice John Marshall. Robert may have already been formulating the position he expressed years later that gradual emancipation was good for white and black alike. But there were seemingly insurmountable practical problems to freeing the slaves. Most of the slaves had no education and no property. How would they earn a living? Where would they live? More important, would they be a threat to society, like Nat Turner and his followers? What if emancipation unleashed thousands of Nat Turners? The nation would descend into bloody chaos and anarchy. And what about the economic loss to the owners? The combined value of slaves in America was on the order of $2 billion (roughly equivalent to $50 billion today; the value of their labor might be ten times that). How could the economy absorb such a jolt?

The Lees went to Arlington for Christmas and enjoyed a wonderful homecoming, a joyous holiday of lavish hospitality and opulent living that were Custis hallmarks. When Robert returned to his duties a month or so later, Mary stayed behind. She had been sick at Ravensworth just after the wedding, and whatever she had then still affected her. By midwinter the river was iced over, giving her an excuse to stay home a little longer. In February she was dangerously ill again, her condition compounded by the fact that she was also pregnant.

Evidently unaware of the details, Robert teased his wife in his letters about reverting to the life of a single man. "Hasten down if you do not want to see me turned out a beau again," he warned. He knew he could never compete with the opulence of Arlington on a lieutenant's pay, but he strongly believed that his family ought to live within its modest means. His father's example was surely in the back of his mind, an example he was determined never to follow. He went on:

> You seem to think, Molly [Mary's nickname], you would pre-
> fer living as we are, but are you right in this? We ought not to
> give others the trouble of providing for us always, and besides
> I can see how we might incommode & be a restraint upon
> them. . . . I know your dear Mother will be for giving you *every*
> thing she has, but must recollect *one* thing, & that is, that they
> have been accustomed to comforts all their life, which now
> they could not dispense with. And that we, in the commence-
> ment, ought to contract our wishes to their smallest compass,
> & enlarge them as opportunity offers.

The letter was like the man: courteous, mindful of others' feelings, determined to do right by everyone, yet clear and persuasive.

After she wrote that she was expecting, his attitude changed completely. "Take care of yourself," he pleaded. "Don't ride on horseback, or go into crowds, or hurry about the house." And she shouldn't go to church for now: "Suppose the carriage was to break down, what would you do then?" Even so, he encouraged her to join him before the summer at Old Point Comfort, on the ocean and away from the steamy tidal marshes of Washington.

Mary finally returned to the fort in June. In the meantime Lee and Captain Talcott agreed to redivide Quarters No. 17—nicknamed the Tuileries as a joke, after the lush royal gardens in Paris—to give the Lees more room. Talcott had married, but his brother-in-law had died; his sister and her children moved out. The Lees took the upstairs and the Talcotts the downstairs. Mrs. Custis arrived along with her daughter, bringing more furniture and two more slaves, then returned home.

When his first child, a healthy son, was born on September 16, 1832, Lieutenant Lee was beside himself. "I have got me an heir to my estates!" the new father wrote to his brother Carter. "Aye, a boy! To cherish the memory of his *father* & walk in the light of his renown!" They named him George Washington Custis Lee. To Robert's relief, Mary recovered quickly and four days later was out riding with him.

Mary had never spent Christmas away from Arlington. Robert wasn't sure his duties would allow him the time off this year, so Mary took their three-month-old son and left Robert alone. When foul weather unexpectedly put an end to construction for a while, Robert dashed after them. Once again they had a festive Christmas, and once again Robert journeyed back to Fort Monroe in January by himself.

The pattern continued for the three years that Lieutenant Lee was stationed at Fort Monroe. Mary spent extended periods with her family, leaving him to pass the time with his friends Andrew Talcott and Joe Johnston. Captain Talcott was away for most of the 1833 building season, making Lieutenant Lee the engineering officer in charge. It was his first opportunity to command. His natural combination of initiative, energy, attention to detail, courtesy, and deference to superiors revealed a leader who could get results because his men wanted to please him, not because they were afraid of him.

On top of his engineering and leadership responsibilities, Lee had to deal with a political battle between the engineers building the fort and the artillerymen who would run it. The artillery units resented the engineers' freedom to sign contracts and disburse money, complained about their quarters on the fort, and believed it was time for them to take charge of the project.

The result was that some engineers would remain at Fort Monroe to work on the foundation breakwaters of huge boulders called ripraps, and that Lee would be in charge. The dust had hardly settled on the new arrangement when the chief engineer of the army, General Charles Gratiot, offered Lee the position as his assistant. Lee's first impulse was to decline the offer. Rearranging boulders was not a prestigious assignment, but it was outdoor work, which he preferred, and he was the officer in charge. For his part, Gratiot recognized Lee's ability and made the office job sound as appealing as possible. Besides, if he worked in Washington, Lee and his family would be only a short ride from the Custis homestead.

In November 1834, to Mary's delight, Robert moved his family to Arlington until he could find lodging for them in Washington. It didn't take long to realize that he could not afford a place there. He didn't think he could live at Arlington because of the odd hours he would have to work. So he took a room alone at Ulrick's Boarding House, where several other young officers lived, and he rode the four miles to Arlington to spend the night when he could.

Living part-time at Ulrick's and part-time at the plantation was something of a disappointment. Lee's new assignment was dreary, too, with day after day of routine paperwork. The drudgery ended when General Gratiot offered Lee the chance to join a surveying expedition marking the disputed boundary between Ohio and Michigan, then a trackless wilderness of rivers and hardwood forests. Trailblazing on the frontier was just the antidote to boring office work.

Mary was expecting again, and she and Robert probably assumed he would be back in Washington by the time the child was due. However, Lee had to wait in New York on surveying tools. That and other delays made it clear he wouldn't be finished with his assignment in time. In those days before the railroads, travel was by steamer, stagecoach, and horseback—unreliable under the best circumstances. Trips were delayed by bad weather, poor roads, high water, availability of horses and forage, and other variables that made it impossible to make firm travel plans.

Nonetheless, Robert looked forward to the trip for the sheer adventure and for the escape from the Washington routine. He was pleased that his friend Captain Talcott would be leaving his current project in New York to command the expedition. Talcott had already surveyed the disputed boundary once.

The team finally arrived at the territorial line and started their work. Isolated as they were, Robert could still exchange letters with Mary. On July 12, 1835, she had a healthy daughter, whom she named Mary Custis, sure beyond a doubt that she would one day be the third Mary to preside as mistress of Arlington House. Robert missed his wife and young family but dutifully threw himself into his responsibilities. His return was postponed time and again, yet he never complained or showed irritation at the delay in meeting his daughter.

In Detroit later that summer, he received a letter from his wife asking him to come home, even if it meant leaving part of his project unfinished. With a newborn in the house, the husband and father should be there. Robert had been gone five months, and there was still no telling when he'd finish his work. She was sure Captain Talcott and General Gratiot would agree that he was needed at home and excuse him to return.

Robert replied with a rare level of irritation and criticism. His duty as a soldier required him to sacrifice time with his family. Rather than answer Mary with his usual empathy and tenderness, he scolded her instead:

> Why do you urge my *immediate* return & tempt one in the strongest manner, to endeavor to get excused from the performance of a duty imposed on me by my profession for the pure gratification of my private feelings? Do you not think that those feelings are enough of themselves to contend with,

without other aggravations; and that I rather require to be strengthened & encouraged to the *full* performance of what I am called to execute, rather than excited to a dereliction, which even our affection could not palliate, or our judgment excuse?

The words rang with a determination to fulfill his duty no matter what the cost and inconvenience to himself or those he loved, a determination never to stumble in doing his duty the way his father had. When it came to a choice between duty to country and duty to family, country came first without question. It was almost as if by comforting his wife, he would be comforting himself, thus showing a lack of resolve and self-sacrifice.

It was October when Lee returned at last to Washington in a season of crisp, cool days and brilliant fall foliage. Dismounting in front of the monumental Arlington portico, he went inside, expecting to welcome both of his Mary Custises. To his surprise, Mr. Custis told him they'd gone to Ravensworth weeks before to escape the muggy Washington summer. Possibly because of the rebuke he'd sent earlier, Mary never told her husband that she had nearly died after their daughter was born.

Robert immediately rode the ten miles to Ravensworth, where he found Mary bedridden, semiconscious, and in constant pain. She'd seemed at first to recover quickly from childbirth, and she was soon walking, riding, and taking on the normal household routine. But soon she developed a fever, lost her appetite, and had to feed her baby with cow's milk from a bottle because she couldn't nurse. Abscesses formed on her inner thighs, probably caused by an infection during childbirth. She hadn't left her bed for weeks and could eat nothing but chicken broth and barley gruel.

Lee immediately had her moved back to Arlington, where he believed Washington doctors could take better care of her. She couldn't even sit up, so she and her bed were loaded into a wagon for the trip home, then gingerly carried by slaves upstairs to her room, where they lifted her out of the Ravensworth bed and into her own.

A week later Robert wrote to Captain Talcott that his wife was "decidedly better." He added, "God grant that it may be the commencement of her recovery." By the end of October, Mary had been treated with warm ointments, leeches, and bleeding, which doctors thought removed "bad blood" responsible for the illness. Once the abscesses were lanced, she could sit up in bed, though she was still too weak to walk. Lee was encouraged by her suddenly ravenous appetite. Mary "gets better every day," he wrote Talcott enthusiastically on November 18. "Her appetite is famous and the partridges, buckwheat muffins & etc. disappear at breakfast as fast as the pheasants, chickens & etc. at dinner." He wrote again in his teasing way when his wife, whose hair was a hopeless tangle after four months in bed, called for a mirror and scissors and cut it off. Her hair, he said, "is now coming out so rapidly that when I left today she talked of having it shaved off, and I expect on my return to find her bald."

The usually magnificent Christmas celebration at Arlington was somewhat subdued that year. Mary recovered slowly and spent part of the season in bed, sometimes watching the festivities from a pallet on the sofa. After the holidays, Robert resumed his work in Washington. On January 8, 1836, Mary wrote in her prayer journal for the first time in twenty-seven months. She thanked God for sparing her life the year before and begged Him to fill her children's hearts with His Spirit. Then she prayed for Robert. Whatever talks they'd had, whatever she had seen of his spiritual character, she was still unsure and concerned about it. "Oh my Father in Heaven," she wrote, "lend an ear to my petitions for those most dear to me. Sad is my heart where they seem more & more indifferent to the things which concern their eternal peace. Why dost Thou withhold from me this blessing?" Two months later, she returned to this burden she carried, praying, "Take my little ones & that loved one of my soul under Thy fatherly care."

Beyond the usual references to God common in polite society, Lieutenant Lee left no record of his spiritual thoughts or struggles during those years. Certainly his character could be described as godly, meaning responsible, attentive, and selfless. He was a hard worker, scrupulously honest and fair, sensitive to others' feelings. These are all attributes associated with Christian character, but not exclusive to it. Lee respected his wife's faith and likely felt a connection with it on some level. But for the present he was focused on his career, his family, and earthly matters that would soon affect the future of both.

Arlington, designed as a living memorial to George Washington by Mary's father, George Washington Parke Custis. Custis grew up at Washington's Mount Vernon estate as the general's foster child. Mary and Robert were married and raised their family here; Mary inherited the property after her father's death. Today it is a national cemetery.

Mary and her youngest son, Robert E. Lee, Jr., taken c. 1845 when the family lived in Brooklyn.

Captain Lee with son William Henry Fitzhugh "Rooney" Lee, possibly taken soon after Lee's return from the Mexican campaign.

Portrait of Lee by Peter A. July & Son, New York, from a photograph taken in the early 1850s by Matthew Brady.

## S I X

# Mississippi Mud

ROBERT WAS CAPTIVATED by children, whether his own
or others, and always gave them special attention. In May 1836
he wrote Captain Talcott about his new arrival:

> The country looks very sweet now . . . and perfumed
> by the blossoms of the trees, the flowers of the garden,
> Honeysuckles, Yellow Jasmine, etc., is more to my taste than
> at any other season of the year. But the brightest flower there
> blooming is my daughter. O, she is a rare one . . . I must
> confess she has, as yet, some little ways about her that do not
> altogether suit a man of my *nervous* temperament.

His wife had scarcely recovered her strength from the complications after Mary's birth when she caught the mumps in June. As
soon as she could travel, Robert took her, the two children, and
four slaves serving as maids and nurses to Warrenton Springs in
the foothills of the Blue Ridge Mountains, about forty miles from
Arlington. A resort had grown up there around mineral springs
that supposedly treated the symptoms of arthritis and other ills.
Guests drank the water and also bathed in it.

Memories of caring for his mother must have flooded back as
he carefully escorted Mary around the grounds and went with her
to the large dining room where all guests shared their meals. On
top of whatever medicinal value the water had, Warrenton Springs
and other places like it gave the region's prominent families a place
to spend the lazy summer days visiting with one another.

Lee may have already had some sense that his wife's health
problems were long term. She was often tired, and he noticed "a
restless anxiety, which renders her unhappy and dissatisfied."
She walked with a limp and showed early signs of rheumatoid
arthritis. A relative who dined often at Arlington and had admired
Lee since his cadet years wrote that in those days, he had always
been "bright, animated, and charming." Seeing the Lees on their
way home from the springs that summer, five years later, she
wrote that Lieutenant Lee "was returning from the Springs with
his wife, who was in distressing ill health, and I never saw a man
so changed and saddened. It has always been painful to me to
think of him as he was then."

Lee's friend Talcott, like numerous other junior officers with
marketable skills, left the military for a better-paying civilian job.

Robert considered resigning his commission to follow their lead. On September 21, after seven years in the army, Lee received his first promotion, to first lieutenant. The better pay would help a little, and Robert decided to stay in the army for the present.

As time allowed, he also helped his father-in-law supervise maintenance on his estate, seeing that fences were repaired and roads maintained. Lee was a loving and affectionate father. Of little Mary, called Mee, he wrote jovially, "Oh she is a rare one, and if only she were sixteen, I would wish myself a *cannibal* that I might eat her up. As it is, I have given all the young ladies a holiday and hurry home to her every day."

He wrote to his brother about Custis, nicknamed Boo or Bourse, and the boy's resolve during his battle with whooping cough: "The *Boo* has the whooping cough, God bless him, but he does not mind—whoops, falls down (not tolerably), gets up, and whoops again."

Before long, Boo and Mee were expecting company. Their mother was due for her third child in the spring of 1837. As if on cue, Robert took another far-off assignment, this time volunteering his services, he told a friend, "to get rid of the office in W[ashington]." This time at least, his departure was delayed until after his new son was born on May 30. They named him William Henry Fitzhugh Lee, nicknamed Rooney from a character in a popular novel.

Robert's new job was technically challenging, and its success was essential in order to keep the American West growing. St. Louis, on the Mississippi River, was the biggest and most important city of the western frontier. The lifeblood of the city was the river, but it was shifting its course and the downtown docks were silting up. St. Louis would soon be landlocked, and the economy would be devastated. Robert's job was to design and build a pier upstream to redirect the river and restore a viable channel.

Lee left for St. Louis in June accompanied by an assistant, Second Lieutenant Montgomery C. Meigs. Years later he wrote that Lee was then "in the vigor of youthful strength, with a noble and commanding presence, and an admirable, graceful and athletic figure. He was one with whom nobody ever wished or ventured to take a liberty, though kind and generous to all his subordinates, admired by all women, and respected by all men. He was the model of a soldier and the beau ideal of a Christian man."

For all its importance, St. Louis didn't impress Lieutenant Lee. In an early letter home he called it "the dearest [most expensive] and dirtiest place I was ever in. Our daily expenses about equal our daily pay." The army was in a rush to get the project going, and Lee went to work right away surveying rapids north of the city, plotting the path of a proposed channel, and examining the threatening sandbars in the commercial district.

Busy as he was, Lieutenant Lee wrote home often, and these letters reveal a change in his attitude since his months in Ohio and Michigan. Soon after arriving, he wrote his wife, "Now that the anxiety and excitement of the journey are over, my thoughts return more forcibly and longingly to all at dear Arlington." In contrast to the stern message he'd sent before, criticizing Mary for tempting him with thoughts of home when she should have known his duty kept him away, his letters from St. Louis were tender and filled with longing for his family and home. Another time he admitted, "I am very anxious, my dear Mary, to get back to see you all.... I dream of you and the dear little children nearly every night."

Later, knowing the family had just come home from a season of extended visits to relations and friends, he wrote of young Custis, "I pray God to watch over and direct our efforts in guarding our dear little son, that we may bring him up in the way he should go.... Oh, what pleasure I lose in being separated from my children! Nothing can compensate me for that; still I must remain here, ready to perform what little service I can, and hope for the best."

He also wrote to the children. Camping beside the Des Moines River during a survey outing, he said on September 10, "Tell Mr. Boo I see plenty of Indians paddling their canoes along the river dressed in all their finery and blankets, and some not dressed at all.... Tell him I can find no ponies, though I see quantities of squirrels, partridges, hares, prairie hens & etc. as I pass along the banks and shores."

For all the effort Lee put into planning the St. Louis project, the city was impatient. Unhappy with the progress he'd made, the city fathers withdrew their portion of the financial support. Lee's only public comment was, "They have a right to do as they wish with their own; I do not own the city. The Government has sent me here as an officer of the army to do a certain work. I shall do it."

Lee's natural leadership ability and unfailing courtesy eventually won the locals over. Mayor John F. Darby later affirmed, Lee "maintained and preserved under all circumstances his dignity and gentlemanly bearing, winning and commanding the esteem, regard and respect of every man under him." The construction office was in an old steamboat moored at the site. Lee sometimes slept aboard to make sure he got an early start.

With winter on the way, Lieutenant Lee could see that he wouldn't be able to begin construction before ice on the river made work impossible. So he shut down for the season and made it home to Arlington for Christmas, traveling part of the way by railroad for the first time. He rode the last leg of the journey from Frederick, Maryland, to Alexandria in a coach of the Baltimore & Ohio Railway, sometimes pulled by a steam engine and sometimes by horses.

Robert had missed his wife and family so much that when time came to return west, he asked Mary and the children to accompany him. St. Louis, though a frontier town, had a population of 15,000 and was growing fast. It would be a safe and relatively comfortable place for the Lee household to live. They decided to make the trip together, but on the date set for their departure, Mee was too sick to travel. Robert was anxious to get to his old steamboat office, so the Lees and their two boys went ahead and Mee stayed with her grandparents. The little girl and her brother Rooney cried for each other at night.

Both boys got sick in Baltimore, and during the ten-day wait for them to recover, Robert and Mary had their portraits painted. Mary had her heart set on Robert sitting in his dress uniform, so she had her mother send it to him. The painter worked on his face until the clothes arrived, then filled in the uniform later. Robert at thirty-one retained his famously straight posture and classic features, still sporting his luxuriant black sideburns all the way down to the jawline. Mary sat for her portrait in a plain but elegant yellow silk dress trimmed in white lace and a shawl of emerald green.

The Lees landed at St. Louis on May 1, 1838, and immediately faced two unpleasant surprises. First, the boat carrying furniture that Robert had bought at a stop in Cincinnati had exploded and sunk. Second, the quarters Lee thought he had arranged for his family were unavailable. He had to scramble to find something else. They made do in temporary rooms for a month, then moved into a house at the corner of Main and Vine that they would share with army surgeon Dr. William Beaumont, his wife, and three children. Dr. Beaumont rented the house from William Clark, one of the leaders of the famous Lewis and Clark expedition.

Rooms there were smaller than Mary was used to, but they were freshly painted and had a sweeping view of the Mississippi. Through the summer, Mary had to deal with children's whooping cough, scarlet fever, and measles and with huge river rats "so numerous that they come up two pair of stairs & make such a noise you would think robbers had got into the house."

Lieutenant Lee tackled his work with customary energy and commitment, building huge dikes to divert the river. He managed military and civilian assistants, contended with local politicians and a press critical of what they considered slow progress, and was prompt and precise in his accounting. The military brass in Washington took note of Lee's outstanding performance. After only a year and eight months as a first lieutenant, he was promoted to captain on August 7.

The new rank and higher pay prompted Lee to wonder again whether he should stay in the army or pursue a civilian engineering career. In a letter written the day he was promoted, he mulled over the matter:

> I do not know whether I ought to rejoice or not . . . as in all my schemes of happiness I look forward to returning to some quiet corner among the hills of Virginia where I can indulge my natural propensities without interruption, and suppose the more comfortably I am fixed in the Army, the less likely I shall be to leave it. As, however, one great cause of my not putting these schemes in execution arises from want of money, I shall in the meantime handle with pleasure the small addition from what [General Gratiot] calls "the tardy promotion."

Lee continued weighing his family's needs and his desire to be with them against his deep-seated sense of duty to country. Besides, it was a perilous time to start a new career. What began as a chain of bank failures in the spring of 1837 had spread across the country, bankrupting businesses and sending unemployment skyrocketing. Even the army felt the economic pressure. Both the local government and the military were wary of voting new appropriations for the St. Louis project.

Mary was expecting again. By the time Robert closed down his work for the season, the river was too icy to travel, and she couldn't take the jostling of so long an overland trip. That meant for the first time in her life, Mary spent Christmas away from home. Once the weather warmed, Lee still had to wait for the river level to fall before he could resume work. So he escorted his wife, eight months pregnant, home in May. It was probably his fastest trip to date, eleven days from start to finish by steamboat to Wheeling, Virginia, and by stagecoach from there home. Robert didn't wait for the new arrival, but returned to St. Louis after only a short rest.

A letter to his wife from Louisville on June 5, 1839, reveals a glimpse of how deeply this reserved young man loved his family. Life as a father had clearly softened his heart. He wrote,

> You do not know how much I have missed you and the children, my dear Mary. To be alone in a crowd is very solitary. In the woods I feel sympathy with the trees and birds, in whose company I take delight, but experience no pleasure in a strange crowd. . . . I . . . must again urge you to be very prudent and careful of those dear children. If I could only get a squeeze at that little fellow [Rooney] turning up his sweet mouth to "keese baba!" You must not let him run wild in my absence, and will have to exercise firm authority over all of them. This will not require severity, or even strictness, but constant attention and an unwavering course. Mildness and forbearance, tempered by firmness and judgment, will strengthen their affection for you, while it will maintain your control over them.

The Lees' fourth child, named Anne Carter Lee after Robert's mother, was born June 18, within days after Captain Lee returned to St. Louis. The child was fine, and this time Mary came through without complications. Her only concern was that Anne had a bright red birthmark on the right side of her face. These marks, called hemangiomas, are usually harmless and often fade away after a few years. Mary fretted when this one didn't fade right away. Robert joked that it was caused by "some *whim wham* of that *Mama*," referring to the old wives' tale that skittish mothers bore abnormal children. Far from worrying or trying to ignore the obvious, Robert nicknamed the new arrival Little Raspberry. In a more reflective mood he wrote his wife, "We must endeavor to assist her to veil if not eradicate [the mark] by the purity and brightness of her mind."

Another season of work passed on the Mississippi. Mayor Darby was impressed by Lee's attitude and seemingly endless reserves of energy. "He went in person with the hands every morning about sunrise," the mayor reported, "and worked day by day in the hot broiling sun. . . . He shared the hard task and common fare and rations furnished to the common laborers,—eating at the same table." When the cold weather came, the laborers were dismissed for the winter, and Robert hurried back to Arlington to meet his six-month-old daughter.

He could scarcely wait to get there. Being separated was "a terrible kind of life," he wrote, "unsatisfactory, profitless & irksome." He added a telling postscript, written beside the address and folded under when the letter was sealed: "I have not mentioned those darling children, not because I have not thought of them, for they are never out of my mind, but it makes me melancholy to think how long it will be before I can see them. Kiss them all for me & don't let them forget me."

Robert relished his time with the children at their grandparents' home that Christmas, becoming "a horse, dog, ladder, and target for cannon." Walking in the woods with Custis, he looked back and noticed the boy stretching to plant his feet in his father's footprints. "It behooves me to walk very straight," Lee said, "when the little fellow is already following in my tracks."

Perhaps Lee discussed his idea of leaving the army with Mr. Custis. The older gentleman hoped someday he'd have Lee's engineering mind and eye for details working on his behalf. Lee figured it would take $20,000 a year to put Arlington "in apple-pie order and make us all comfortable," but he didn't have that kind of money. He suspected Mr. Custis didn't either.

Spring 1840 found Robert still waiting for orders to return to his project, halted for lack of appropriations, and meanwhile filling in at the chief engineer's office as before. After Congress adjourned for the summer without allocating any money to Lee's work, his Washington superiors discussed postponing the job for a year or two. But maintaining the expensive equipment while it sat idle was too costly, so in July, Robert returned to St. Louis to sell the work boats and equipment at a public auction.

On this trip west, Lee felt even more lonesome than usual because the work into which he had put so much effort was coming to a halt unfinished. Going out for some air one night, he saw a captivating sight that he shared with Mary in a letter on September 4, 1840:

> Feeling lonesome, as the saying is, and out of sorts, I got on a
> horse and took a ride. On returning through the lower part of
> the town, I saw a number of little girls all dressed up in their
> white frocks & pant[alet]s & hair plaited and tied up with
> ribands, running and chasing each other in all directions. I
> counted 23 nearly the same size. As I drew up my horse to

admire the spectacle a man appeared at the door with the 24th in his arms.

The man explained that the children were there for a party, though he wished they all had been his. Lee added in his letter, "I do not think the eldest exceeded 7 or 8 years old. It was the prettiest sight I have seen in the West, and perhaps in my life."

The more children he had, the more tenderhearted for them he seemed to become. Lee number five, Eleanor Agnes, was born February 27, 1841, only twenty months after her sister Anne. Soon and from then on, the two were referred to as "the girls," while older sister Mary was "Daughter," short for "daughter Mary" to differentiate her from her mother and her grandmother.

During his three and a half years in Missouri, Robert matured from a capable but unknown and unproven junior engineer into a captain with exemplary engineering skills and impressive leadership ability. He was marked as a rising young star. Unfortunately for Robert, the same budget crisis that closed down his St. Louis assignment early meant there were few other engineering opportunities. After another short stint in Washington, he went on an inspection tour of East Coast forts. In early 1841 he was offered his choice between supervising repairs of forts he'd surveyed in North Carolina or repairing and upgrading fortifications in New York Harbor. Of the two, Captain Lee figured New York was far more important and, he hoped, more interesting.

## SEVEN

# Building in Brooklyn

NEW YORK IN 1841 was already the largest city in the United States, a center of finance and commerce, and a vital terminal for ocean traffic to and from Europe. More than half a million people lived in the area, though much of the region outside Manhattan Island was still sparsely populated. Captain Lee's assignment there was to design and build improvements to two forts and two artillery batteries in the harbor. The forts, Hamilton and Lafayette, were at the Narrows, two points of land that pinched the harbor into upper and lower divisions. Fort Hamilton was on the eastern shore in Brooklyn, and Lafayette on a reef just off-shore. The Hudson and Morton Batteries were on Staten Island.

Robert arrived on April 10 and decided his family should live at Fort Hamilton. Brooklyn, Lee observed, was uncrowded, with lots of trees and "quantities of handsome country seats in all directions." He found quarters for his wife and five children on the fort and wanted to have the place painted and refurbished, though he teased Mary that "a nice yankee wife would soon have it in fine order." Ever frugal, Robert had sold their St. Louis furniture rather than ship it back east. Now he sent for goods they'd had in storage since they left Fort Monroe. Mrs. Custis gave Mary more furnishings, and Robert said they could buy the rest in New York, though he warned, "they show you so many handsome things that it is dangerous to go in the stores."

At the last minute, the rooms that Robert had in mind were commandeered for officers, and the Lees had to move into a rented house nearby. Neighbors were curious about the slaves that Mary had to keep house and take care of the children. Slavery had been outlawed in New York in 1827, but as citizens of a slaveholding state, the Lees had a right to their property, just as if they'd been in Virginia. Robert joked to Mary that some of their new acquaintances had "misgivings as to whether you possess all your faculties, having so much help under foot."

After years off and on as a long-distance parent, the captain delighted in having his family with him. He still worried that his wife didn't discipline the children enough. He even wrote Mrs. Custis for help in convincing Mary that she needed to be stricter. "It requires much earnestness," he explained, "to induce her to conform to what she is not herself impressed with the necessity of. . . . [D]iscipline will be too lax, too inconsistent, too yielding." He requested, "*Make* her do what is right."

The five years Captain Lee spent in Brooklyn were some of

the happiest of his life. As in St. Louis, the work was unexciting and chronically underfunded, but it was important to the nation and there was a variety of jobs to do: repairing leaks, modifying gun mounts, refinishing the floors and ceilings of the magazines and building new ones, adding shot furnaces to the batteries, extending parapet walls, and more. Mary enjoyed the longest stretch of good health she'd had since Daughter was born. She went shopping, dazzled by the variety, opulence, and high prices of New York goods. She rode horseback, and when she took the children swimming, she often swam with them. She met other Virginians living in Brooklyn and shared with them the flower and vegetable seeds her mother sent from Arlington. Mary planted lush gardens around their house, noting that the season for everything lagged several weeks behind what she was used to at home.

Besides being a comfortable place, New York had the location and the means of transportation to make the trip back to Arlington an easy one. Mary could come and go almost as she pleased, taking various combinations of children with her and leaving the rest with their father. They spent every Christmas but one at the estate during those years. Mr. Custis carried on as always with his grand hospitality, decorating the sideboard with Mount Vernon silver and dishes, including a huge punchbowl with a figure of a ship on the inside. Tradition dictated that when the punch was drunk down to the bottom of the masts, it was time to turn in.

During the fall of 1843, Mary returned to Arlington to give birth to her sixth child, a boy born on October 27 and named Robert Edward Lee Jr. When his father finally met him that winter, he observed that his namesake "has a fine long nose like his father, but no whiskers."

At a time when child mortality was commonplace, the Lees were fortunate that all of their children were alive and reasonably healthy. There had been a scare, though, sometime between their move to New York and now when Annie, her father's Little Raspberry, got hold of a pair of scissors and, before anyone knew what was happening, pierced her right eyeball. Lee had said earlier that her sterling character and disposition would offset the physical blemish of her birthmark. No doubt he was equally philosophical about her wound, and Mary was predictably frantic and devastated. Annie was blinded in that eye and permanently disfigured.

In the summer of 1843 Lee was ordered to West Point to suggest a site for a new barracks. It was the first time he had been on campus since his graduation and commissioning in 1829, and it gave him a chance to see what changes had been made in the tradition-bound institution during his fourteen years in uniform. He was back again for two weeks the next summer to monitor final exams. During this time he visited with old acquaintances from his cadet days, including his cadet commander Major Worth, now a brevet brigadier.

The most important figure he met during that 1844 trip was Major General Winfield Scott. General Scott was an imposing six feet five inches tall, and his love of military display and decorum had earned him the nickname "Old Fuss and Feathers." He was a revered military leader, a battle veteran in a time when few of them were in the service. He had received his commission personally from President Thomas Jefferson in 1808, and he had been taken prisoner during the War of 1812.

Probably Lee and Scott had met before, since both men spent so much time at army headquarters in Washington, but this was when they got to know each other and when Scott identified Captain Lee as a sterling officer worthy of special notice. Despite the difference in their ages, ranks, and experience, their time together cemented a valuable friendship that would have historic consequences.

The year passed quietly for Lee in New York. But as Mary prepared to return home for Christmas 1845, there was another family crisis. Thirteen-year-old Custis was at school in Virginia, Daughter was with her grandparents, and Mary was eager to get home ahead of the arrival of her seventh child, expected in February. On November 24, while she was at a neighbor's saying good-bye and Robert was at work, eight-year-old Rooney wandered into the barn and sliced off the tips of two fingers on his left hand with a straw cutter—the index finger at the root of the nail and the middle finger at the first joint. Hearing his screams, a slave rushed in, retrieved the fingertips, sent for Mrs. Lee, and went with them to the post infirmary. Rooney bore the pain manfully, and once the doctor finished sewing, his parents took turns sitting up all night with him to make sure the fingers stayed protected.

Rooney couldn't travel for weeks, so the family was separated at Christmas, with the two oldest children away and the rest spending their first Christmas in New York. The fingertips failed to mend, though to a casual observer, Rooney's fingers seemed normal. Hoping to turn tragedy into a useful lesson, Captain Lee wrote to his son Custis on November 30: "See how two have been punished for their inattention & disobedience. One with the loss of an eye, another with the amputation of two fingers. If children could know the misery, the desolating sorrow, with which their acts sometimes overwhelm their parents, they could not have the heart thus cruelly to affect them."

It was perhaps a lot to expect of young children that they were old enough to see the danger in what they were doing, and awfully stern to accuse them of somehow doing such things on purpose. A model of consistency, Lee displayed compassion and yet also underscored the importance of rules and self-control, even for a three-year-old with scissors.

Mary's Christmas Day letter to her mother paints a picture of a very active household, and a happy but tired mother keeping track of four young children while seven months pregnant with another. Captain Lee filled the children's stockings, which they woke up to explore while it was still dark outside. It was, Mary wrote, "a day of great enjoyment to the young ones." She continued:

> The children were awake at 4 o-clock this morning discussing the contents of their stockings & could not be induced to sleep again so that I feel pretty tired tonight. . . . I have felt sad that we could not all be together, but thankful that our young ones were all well & Rooney well enough to accompany us to Col. Staunton's where we dined.
>
> The ground is covered with snow but not deep & the weather quite mild. I took Annie & Wig [Agnes] to church, which

was beautifully decorated with evergreens. Mr. Gardner gave
us a very good sermon & then administered the communion.

Rob is standing by the table & says I must tell Grandma
to get him . . . a carriage & horses . . . very moderate requests.

Assuming they would be in New York for a long time, Mrs.
Lee had moved her membership from the church in Alexandria,
where she had worshiped all her life, to the small Episcopal parish
church at Fort Hamilton. Captain Lee had never formally joined
the church, though surely he and Mary had continued talking
about it as they had earlier in their marriage. Every morning at
Arlington after breakfast, Mrs. Custis led a devotional time with
prayers, which Mary wholeheartedly participated in while her
father often snoozed quietly. Like Robert, Mr. Custis had never
had any formal connection with the church, though he invoked
divine blessings in his conversations and frequent public speeches.

Robert was genuinely respectful of religion, however deep his
personal feelings went. Though he had never been confirmed, he
was a lay leader in the Fort Hamilton church, which was also the
post chapel. One of Lee's fellow officers reported that the Lee family "formed a charming portion of our little society" and that Lee
"was a vestryman of the little parish church of Fort Hamilton, of
which the post-chaplain was the rector, and as thorough in the discharge of church as of other duties." Because of Lee's position as a
captain and vestryman, both sides in any congregational disagree-
ment tried to enlist his support. True to form, unless the matter
involved honesty or honor—and they never did, but were matters
of practice and preference—Lee held a diplomatic middle ground.

Rooney's fingers were healed well enough to travel by January, and on February 10, 1846, at the age of thirty-seven, Mary gave birth at Arlington to her seventh and final child, named Mildred Childe Lee after Robert's sister living in Paris. In a familiar routine, Mary stayed at Arlington to recover while her husband returned to his duties in New York. On May 3 he wrote encouraging her to leave the Washington heat and get back to him as soon as she felt able: "I hope you will make your trip up the country at once and then come on as soon after as you can. I am very lonesome & solitary & want to see you all very much. Besides, those 'chillen' can't do without their Papa." He was also anxious to meet the newest of his "chillen," to kiss her "fragrant mouth & feel that little heart fluttering against mine."

Mary was packing up for Brooklyn when she heard that Congress had declared war on Mexico. She knew Robert was busy with a strategically important engineering assignment and that, as an engineering staff officer, he wouldn't be called to fight right away, if ever. Yet she also knew her husband's disposition and his heart. Promotion and opportunity and honor were rare on a construction site, but plentiful on the battlefield. The U.S. Army hadn't fought in combat in almost two generations, since the Battle of New Orleans in 1814. Robert would want to be in the thick of it.

# EIGHT

## The Very Best

THE PROSPECT OF war with Mexico had simmered since 1836. That year Texas won its independence and signed a treaty establishing the Rio Grande as the border between the two nations. When Texas joined the Union nine years later, the river became the boundary between the United States and Mexico. Yet according to Mexico, the man who negotiated the treaty on its behalf, General Antonio López de Santa Anna, wasn't authorized to make the agreement. The boundary, the Mexicans claimed, was actually the Nueces River well to the north, cutting off the whole southern tip of the state.

When President James K. Polk sent former Louisiana Congressman John Slidell as his personal minister plenipotentiary to try and buy California and New Mexico from Mexico for $25 million, the authorities refused to receive him, claiming a state of war existed between the U.S. and Mexico over Texas. In response, President Polk sent General Zachary Taylor to secure the land between the Nueces and the Rio Grande. When a scouting party was killed by Mexican soldiers, Polk asked Congress for a declaration of war.

As Mary suspected, Captain Lee would never be content building forts in New York Harbor if there was a war to fight. On May 12, 1846, he wrote to her at Arlington, where she was still recuperating from Mildred's birth, admitting his doubts about America's justification for war. To him it seemed as though the United States was the aggressor, but he vowed to do his part nonetheless. "I wish I was better satisfied as to the justice of our cause," he said, "but that is not my providence to consider, & should my services be wanted I shall promptly furnish them."

The next day the United States declared war on Mexico. Within a month, Captain Lee asked Colonel Joseph G. Totten, his superior as chief engineer, for a transfer to the battlefront: "In the event of war with any foreign government I should desire to be brought into active service in the field with as high a rank in the regular army as I could obtain. If that could not be accomplished without leaving the Corps of Engineers, I should then desire a transfer."

Robert and Mary decided she should stay at Arlington until it was clear whether he would be leaving New York. On August 19, Robert received orders to report to Brigadier General John E. Wool in San Antonio, Texas, for duty in Mexico. After seventeen years in uniform, Lee was heading for his first taste of combat.

Lee made his will on August 31. Probably he had never spent

any of the small legacy that his mother's estate had left him. He'd put that money in St. Louis city bonds and other safe investments yielding about $2,000 per year, which more than doubled his military salary and allowances of about $1,300 annually. (This totaled a modern equivalent of around $90,000, a comfortable income but not lavish for a couple with seven children.) He left his entire estate to his wife for the rest of her life; at her death it would be divided equally among the children, except an extra amount for Annie, whom he thought would need it because of her partial blindness.

Captain Lee said good-bye to his wife and children, not knowing when he would see them again. Mr. Custis was proud to see his son-in-law taking up arms in defense of his country, and he presented Lee with George Washington's camp knife and fork to carry during the campaign. Days later the captain was on his way, riding the train to Wheeling, Virginia, then by steamer to New Orleans. Traveling with his Irish orderly, Jim Connally, and a group of volunteer soldiers, and carrying $60,000 from the War Department to General Wool, Lee sailed from New Orleans to Port Lavaca, Texas, and rode horseback inland to San Antonio, where he arrived September 21.

A week later, General Wool's column was ordered to the Rio Grande and then westward toward the city of Chihuahua, while General Zachary Taylor and his men marched south from the river toward Monterey. Clearing a path for Wool's command of nearly two thousand men, the "indefatigable exertions of those distinguished officers" of the engineering corps built bridges and prepared the way for troops heading to the river. On October 12, they forded the wide but shallow Rio Grande and became invaders on foreign soil.

The next several months consisted of weeks of idle time interrupted by bursts of frantic activity based on rumors of enemy action, as Captain Lee experienced at Christmas that year. On Christmas Eve, Robert wrote to his wife and children at Arlington, imagining the wonderful family celebration they were enjoying. Emotions welled up inside as he recorded his thoughts:

> We have had many happy Christmases together & this is the first time we have been entirely separated at this holy time since our marriage. I hope it does not interfere with your happiness, surrounded as you are by father, mother, children, and dear friends. I therefore trust that you are well and happy, and that this is the last time I shall be absent from you during my life. May God preserve & bless you till then & forever after is my constant prayer.

He also sent cheerful letters to Custis and Rooney:

> I hope good Santa Claus will fill my Rob's stockings tonight, & that Mildred's, Agnes' & Anna's may break down with good things. I do not know what he will have for you & Mary, but if he only leaves you half of what I wish you, you will want for nothing. I have frequently thought if I had one of you on each side of me riding on ponies, such as I could get you, I would be comparatively happy.

At an impromptu Christmas dinner for the commanding officers, Lee set George Washington's knife and fork at General Wool's place, and he happily informed Mary that they were "passed around the table with much veneration & excited universal attention."

In contrast to so peaceful an interlude, the next morning brought word of a possible attack. Captain Lee volunteered to scout the situation and was assigned a local guide and a cavalry escort. Somehow he missed the cavalry rendezvous, but went ahead without them. When he and his guide saw campfires on a hillside, Lee's young Mexican companion warned him to turn back or face capture. The guide retreated and Lee proceeded solo, discovering that the fire belonged to a group of shepherds. In halting Spanish he asked them for information on troop movements and, based on what he learned, rode back to headquarters for a fresh horse and his cavalry outriders. The second time out he returned to report that there was no threat to the Americans. Partly because of Lee's volunteer scouting mission, General Wool appointed him acting inspector general.

Scarcely three weeks after his scouting sortie, Captain Lee received orders to join the command of General Winfield Scott. The general in chief of the army was leading a huge invasion force toward Veracruz, the largest port in Mexico, and from there inland to take the capital, Mexico City. On February 19, Lee stepped ashore with the general to the kind of rousing display of bugles and banners that Old Fuss and Feathers so appreciated. On the twenty-seventh, he wrote a long letter to his sons describing his adventures:

I have been to Tampico. I saw many things to remind me of you, though that was not necessary to make me wish that you were with me. The river was so calm and beautiful, and the boys were playing about in their boats, and swimming their ponies. . . . We had a grand parade on General Scott's arrival. . . . There were six thousand soldiers. . . .

I have a nice state-room on board this ship; Joe Johnston and myself occupy it, but my poor Joe is so sick all the time I can do nothing with him. . . . Vessels were expressly fitted up for the horses, and parties of dragoons detailed to take care of them. . . . I took every precaution for their comfort, provided them with bran, oats, etc., and had slings made to pass under them and attached to the coverings above, so that, if in a heavy sea they should slip, or be thrown off their feet, they could not fall. . . .

Tell Rob he must think of me very often, be a good boy, and always love papa. . . . The ship rolls so that I can scarcely write. You must write to me very often. I am always very glad to hear from you. Be sure that I am thinking of you, and that you have the prayers of your affectionate father, R. E. Lee.

Cruising offshore Veracruz about a week later, Lee was invited along with General Scott and the rest of his staff to scout the coast for landing points with Commodore David Conner. The port had been blockaded by the American navy for weeks, and the Mexicans still manned the castle fort of San Juan d'Ulloa guarding the approach by sea to the city. About a mile and a half from shore, the officers' boat was fired upon, but the shot was wide. A soldier for eighteen years then, Lee heard his first enemy gun.

Scott chose a sandy beach three miles down the shore from Veracruz for his invasion and ordered everything prepared for a landing the next day, March 9. The infantry division led by Scott's friend and former aide General William Worth was the vanguard of a massive amphibious invasion. The sight of the ships, Worth's landing, and the landing of thousands of troops drew no enemy fire. Their action was unopposed.

General Scott gathered a group of trusted officers to discuss what to do next. They could attack, or they could lay siege to the fort. This "kitchen cabinet," as Scott called it, included several promising young officers who would play a part in Captain Lee's future: his friend Joe Johnston, Second Lieutenant George B. McClellan, First Lieutenant P. G. T. Beauregard, and George Gordon Meade. Lee also met another skilled junior officer named Thomas Jonathan Jackson, who would one day become one of his closest and most trusted friends.

The army brought the rest of its huge force ashore and prepared for a siege, digging earthworks and positioning heavy guns borrowed from the navy. On March 19, Lee was nearly killed walking back to the lines from inspecting a forward position with Lieutenant Beauregard. A skittish American soldier thought he was a Mexican and fired at him with his pistol. The bullet passed between Lee's left arm and his side, singeing his uniform.

The Mexicans finally opened fire on the invaders' battery on March 24, but their shots were ineffective. Lee directed fire from the entrenched American position, his first experience in combat. After exchanging fire for two days, the Mexicans sent out a white flag during a raging sandstorm. A day later, the fortress surrendered.

General Scott planned to press on toward Mexico City in search of the main body of the Mexican army. The general in chief of Mexican forces and sometime president of Mexico, General Santa Anna, had already lost the Battle of Buena Vista to Generals Zachary Taylor and John E. Wool, even though the Mexican army was three times as large as the invading force. Santa Anna had retreated into the interior to reorganize. By mid-April, Scott and his troops had reached the Rio del Plan, where Santa Anna and his men waited for them in a secure mountain pass beyond a crest called Cerro Gordo.

General Scott ordered Lee to see if there was a way around the pass. Picking his way around the left side, Lee decided that though the terrain was treacherous, a road could be cleared for the soldiers. The army moved out on April 17 with Lee as their scout. The next day Scott's men attacked. Lee continued around the Mexican position to cut off their escape. Though General Santa Anna slipped through, three thousand of his men were captured, along with thousands of rifles and most of their artillery. While Santa Anna escaped, his artificial leg of leather-covered cork did not. The Fourth Illinois Infantry surprised him while he was having a meal, forcing him to mount his horse and gallop away and leave his leg and other personal items behind.

Writing on April 27 to his brother Smith, whose naval unit was also fighting in the war, Lee told the story with scant regard for his critical part in the action or the danger he faced:

> On the 17th I led General Twigg's division in the rear of a hill
> in front of Cerro Gordo, and in the afternoon, when it became

necessary to construct a battery at night, the first intimation of our presence or intentions was known. . . . Soon after sunrise our batteries opened, and I started with a column to turn their left. . . . Not withstanding their efforts to prevent us in this, we were perfectly successful, and the working party, following our footsteps, cut out the road for the artillery. In the meantime our storming party had reached the crest of Cerro Gordo, and, seeing their whole left turned and the position of our soldiers . . . they broke and fled. Those in the pass laid down their arms.

Captain Lee's first battlefield engagement brought a sobering realization of the inhumanity and brutality of war. "You have no idea what a horrible sight a field of battle is," he wrote to his fourteen-year-old son Custis. Lee surely thought of his children when he went into town after the battle and saw a girl standing beside a wounded drummer boy, perhaps her brother, pinned under the body of a dying soldier. To Mary, hundreds of miles and a world away in the lush elegance of Arlington, he described the scene: "Her large black eyes were streaming with tears, her hands crossed over her breast; her hair in one long plait behind reached her waist, her shoulders and arms bare, and without stockings or shoes. Her plaintive tone of '*Mille gracias, Signor,*' as I had the dying man lifted off the boy and both carried to the hospital, still lingers in my ears."

Lee's actions raised him still higher in General Scott's eyes. In his account of the Battle of Cerro Gordo, the general reported, "I am impelled to make special mention of the services of Captain R. E. Lee, engineers. This officer, greatly distinguished at the

siege of Vera Cruz, was again indefatigable during these operations, in reconnaissance as daring as laborious, and of the utmost
value. Nor was he less conspicuous in planting batteries, and in
conducting columns to their stations under the heavy fire of the
enemy." As Lee biographer Douglas Southall Freeman noted,
"No other officer of the army received such high praise."

Frustrated at the Mexican general's continued retreat toward
Mexico City, Scott had to wait for new soldiers before he could
chase him. Many of the regular troops had enlisted for three
months at the beginning of the war. Most were ready to go home,
so the army had to wait for their replacements to be trained and
sent to central Mexico. Not only was the delay difficult for Scott,
it gave Santa Anna time to regroup and replace his casualties. Lee
kept himself busy drilling the men and preparing a map of the
recommended approach to Mexico City.

The road to the capital ran on a narrow causeway westward
through marshes between Lake Texcoco on the north and Lakes
Xochimilco and Chalco on the south. General Worth wanted to
take his division south of Lake Chalco, then pick up the Acapulco
Road that ran north through the town of Churubusco, along the
east side of an almost impenetrable lava field called a pedregal.
The San Angel Road ran along the west side of the pedregal,
then joined the Acapulco Road at Churubusco. Continuing up
the Acapulco Road meant the U.S. forces would have to face a
heavily fortified position. If they could somehow get around the
southern margin of the pedregal, they could take the San Angel
Road all the way to Churubusco. From there they had a clear path
to Mexico City.

At night, groping his way through a violent thunderstorm, Lee scouted the southern edge of the pedregal, picking his way over huge boulders and treacherous chasms, guided only by flashes of lightning. He came across General James Shields's men trying to join General Persifor Smith's and led them to Smith's position. He took a message to Scott from Smith, hoping to coordinate an attack. After three impossible miles, Lee arrived at Scott's location only to learn the general had left. He stumbled three more miles before finding the general at last. Scott was happy to see Lee not only because the captain had survived a dangerous assignment, but also because he had sent seven messengers to find General Smith and none of them had succeeded.

The army made a pair of successful attacks, and Lee fought in both after his long scramble over the pedregal, going thirty-six hours without sleep. The Mexicans asked for a truce, and General Scott and his men halted about a mile from Chapultepec, the main defense complex on the western outskirts of Mexico City. The general, in typical fashion, set up his headquarters in the bishop's palace on a hillside.

Chapultepec was a ridge six hundred yards long, fortified by a massive stone building. This fortress guarded the entrance to the causeway through a swamp and into the streets of Mexico City. On September 7, the truce ended with no movement toward a permanent agreement, and Scott huddled with his "kitchen cabinet" of advisors, including Lee, to settle on a plan of action. Despite the strong Mexican position, Scott and his officers decided to try and take the high ground of Chapultepec, giving them the straight causeways over the marsh. Still without sleep, Lee assisted General

Scott, moving back and forth between units and coordinating the attack. He was also in charge of building four batteries to fire on Chapultepec. Lee helped explain the plan to other generals, then guided General Gideon Pillow's troops into position. Scott sent Lee to scout approaches to one of the main city gates. During his ride, he got a slight wound, but didn't stop to have it dressed. He returned to General Scott at Chapultepec, rode with him on the line of General Worth's advance, and then, exhausted beyond all limits, fainted for the only time in his life.

On September 14, 1847, a delegation of townspeople came to Scott's headquarters to say Santa Anna had retreated and the city was theirs. General Scott and his men, in full dress uniforms, marched into the city as conquerors.

It was the next April before all the details of the treaty were settled, and Lee spent those months making new maps of Mexico City, the surrounding terrain, and the battlefields.

Due largely to General Scott's effusive praise, Lee received a string of brevet promotions in short order, culminating with the rank of colonel on September 13. Years later Scott would write that Lee in action in Mexico was "the very best soldier that I ever saw in the field."

# NINE

# Commandant

VETERANS OF THE Mexican War poured into Washington by the boatload. In the early summer of 1848, wave after wave of suntanned soldiers marched festively from Georgetown to Arlington Spring for their homecoming celebrations. The little ferry steamer carried a steady stream of picnickers to the spot as families welcomed their husbands and fathers home.

Brevet Colonel Robert E. Lee was not in the happy crowd, however. The commander of occupation forces, General William Orlando Butler, had requested that Lee stay behind to assist him. Mrs. Lee went to see General Scott in Washington, who repeated his high praise for her husband and said he would get him back for her. Expecting Robert home on June 29, Mary laid out his favorite summer clothes freshly washed and pressed, a special treat after

89

twenty-one months in uniform. She and the children dressed in their Sunday best. Custis was nearly sixteen now and talking of a military career; daughter Mary was two weeks shy of thirteen; eleven-year-old Rooney was still the high-spirited rabble-rouser; Annie and Agnes, nine and seven, were best friends; Rob, four, scarcely remembered his father; Mildred, two, didn't remember him at all.

Mr. Custis sent his coach to the train station, and the family took turns the rest of the afternoon watching for it on the drive. Robert didn't expect anyone to meet him, so he set out from the depot on horseback. He walked into the front hall to see his children lined up waiting, almost bursting with excitement. As they ran to hug him, he scooped up little Mildred in his arms. He wouldn't have recognized her and in fact didn't recognize Rob. Picking up a child to give him a welcoming embrace, Robert discovered he was a neighbor boy on a visit with his mother. Mrs. Lee waited at the back of the hall until all the children had a moment with their father, then hurried into his arms.

After so long away, Lee made a special effort to reconnect with his family. Rob and Mildred were shy around this stranger for a while, but soon warmed to him. Mary noticed that his face was more lined and that he had the first flecks of gray in his hair. He'd added a moustache to his side whiskers before leaving for Mexico, but shaved both off during the campaign, even though Mary thought them "exceedingly becoming." Some mornings the children would come into their parents' room, climb into bed with them, and cuddle up for a story from Papa. On days when he didn't go into his job at army headquarters in Washington, Lee played outside with them and let them crawl over Grace Darling, the horse he'd brought back with him. He told them of her bravery and showed them her seven round scars, one for each time she'd been shot by a Mexican soldier.

At night the family gathered in front of the fire to hear Papa tell about his travels, though he seldom mentioned his battlefield experiences. He read aloud from Walter Scott, holding the same books in the same room where he had once courted their mother. As payment for reading, Lee playfully insisted the children take turns tickling his feet. When the tickler stopped—drawn into the story or fallen asleep—Lee abruptly quit reading and declared with mock seriousness, "No tickling, no reading!" Sundays they drove to Christ Church in Alexandria, where they always sat in Robert's favorite spot, in the gallery to the left of the pulpit.

General Zachary Taylor was elected president in the fall of 1848. Around the time Taylor was voted in, Colonel Lee was posted to Baltimore to build a new fort on Sollers Point Flats. He reported for duty on November 18, 1848, but couldn't start work because no money was allocated and the weather was already turning foul. Lee and Taylor maintained a cordial friendship, and the next May, Colonel and Mrs. Lee dined with President Taylor at the Executive Mansion, the men swapping stories of the Mexican War late into the night.

Earlier that spring, in April 1849, Lee went back to Baltimore to start his project and find a house for his family. There would soon be only six children at home. Custis wanted to go to West Point, and Mary's Aunt Eleanor—Mr. Custis's sister, who'd grown up with him at Mount Vernon—asked her good friend the president to appoint him. President Taylor replied in part, "The son of Col. Lee, whose father has done so much in Mexico in contributing to our success there, and who deservedly stands so high with all who knew him as a soldier, a man and a gentleman, is unquestionably entitled . . . to an appointment at the Military Academy."

The family's new home in Baltimore was a townhouse owned by Lee's uncle William Wickham. The place was small and dark, one room wide, four rooms deep, and three stories high with the classic marble Baltimore steps out front. His and his wife's bedroom was "hardly big enough to swing a cat in," he said, but they would make do. The house was still under construction when Robert started work, so from April until October he traveled back and forth, the trip to Alexandria now an easy journey by train. During a visit to Arlington in July, Lee caught malaria and moved to the higher ground of Ravensworth to recuperate. It was the first recorded sickness of his life, and it kept him down for a month.

Robert suggested that they not bring any slaves with them. Baltimore was a hotbed of abolitionist activity, and though the Custis slaves were by all accounts well treated, Robert was afraid they would pick up radical ideas that could cause problems then or later. In the end they took one servant, a nurse named Eliza.

Mary and Robert enjoyed a rare season of calm during their years in Baltimore. Custis stayed in school in Alexandria until his appointment came through, then moved to New York, but the rest of the family were together and happy. There were the usual traumas and sickness—four in the family had the measles at once—but in many ways they were serene days.

Robert's sister Anne lived in Baltimore with her husband, Judge William Marshall, a former U.S. district attorney there. Like Washington, Baltimore was a place where social connections made all the difference, and Judge and Mrs. Marshall knew everybody, including Jerome Bonaparte Jr., a nephew of Napoleon. The Lees loved parties, visits, and evenings at the theater, and they mixed comfortably with the cream of Baltimore society. Years later Rob recalled his parents' frequent nights out. His father was "always in full uniform, always ready and waiting for my mother, who was generally late. He would chide her gently, in a playful way and with a bright smile. He would then bid us good-bye, and I would go to sleep with this beautiful picture in my mind, the golden epaulets and all—chiefly the golden epaulets."

Meanwhile, President Taylor was contending more frequently with the issue of slavery in the West. Some fellow Southerners called him a turncoat for not actively promoting slavery in newly forming territories and states. California wanted to be admitted as a free state, but much of it was south of the Missouri Compromise line where slavery was legal. Slave owners and their supporters didn't want such a big expanse of Southern land to be free. Taylor had no patience with radical proslavery proponents any more than he did with people trying to abolish slavery where it was allowed. He resolved to enforce the federal law and preserve the Union, and he said he would lead an army if necessary. He said he would hang anyone "taken in rebellion against the Union" with "less reluctance" than he had hanged spies and deserters during the Mexican War.

On Independence Day 1850, President Taylor attended

a ceremony in Washington where G. W. P. Custis dedicated a stone from the people of Washington to the construction of the Washington Monument. The day was blazing hot, and the president ate heartily from the picnic spread before him. Five days later he was dead, probably of gastroenteritis caused by bacteria. Taylor died without making Custis Lee's appointment to the military academy, but his successor, Millard Fillmore, sent it forward.

Returning to Baltimore from a visit to Custis at West Point in April 1851, Lee later wrote him that he had a surprising homecoming. In Baltimore the Lees entertained visitors as they always had, even though the house was much smaller than they were used to. Arriving by train before dawn, Lee climbed the stairs to his room and was met by Mary at the bedroom door. Her cousin Emma Randolph was sleeping in his spot. He quietly walked down the hall. In the next room cousin Cornelia Randolph was sleeping with Daughter; past them, little Mildred had moved in with Rob and Rooney. All the master of the house could do was doze in a chair until breakfast.

Lee spent his time just as he had in St. Louis and New York, planning and building fortifications, and putting up with repeated bureaucratic delays in funding. Every day he took the horse-drawn public bus from his house on Madison Avenue to the wharf. Two oarsmen waited there to row him across the harbor in a small boat, first to his project headquarters at Sollers Point and later to the construction site on the tidal flats beyond.

Colonel Lee continued dutifully with his work into the spring of 1852, driving piles and laying stone for the foundations of Fort Carroll. On May 28, taken completely by surprise, he was directed to transfer his command to one of his subordinates "in order that you may proceed to West Point toward the close of the month of August and on the 1st of September next relieve Capt. Brewerton of the Superintendency of the Military Academy, and of the command of the post of West Point." Secretary of War Charles M. Conrad would have asked for recommendations from General Scott, who held Lee in highest regard, and from Colonel Totten, whom Lee had served so admirably.

It was a plum assignment, arguably the most prestigious command in the Corps of Engineers, and one of only a handful of shining opportunities for a staff officer. Colonel Lee felt unqualified for the transfer. He likely dreaded the thought of politics and paperwork after tasting action on the battlefield. In typical fashion he thought nothing about the prestige of the opportunity or about his personal dislike of administrative work, but about what was best for the institution and its students. For the only documented time in his long career, Lee questioned an order from his superior. He wrote back to Colonel Totten:

> I learn with much regret the determination of the Secretary of War to assign me to that duty, and I fear I cannot realize his expectations in the management of an Institution requiring more skill and more experience than I can command.
>
> Although fully appreciating the honor of the station, and extremely reluctant to oppose my wishes to the orders of the Department, yet if I be allowed any option in the matter, I would respectfully ask that some other successor than myself be appointed to the present able Superintendent.

The secretary evidently took Lee's request seriously because it was more than a week before Lee received a reply. At last he got word that the decision would stand, and Lee would become commandant of the military academy on September 1. Ever attentive to the last detail, Lee turned his perfectly balanced accounts over to his replacement in Baltimore on August 21 and, two days later, traveled up the Hudson to his next duty station.

The new commandant soon realized that his students were coming to the academy unprepared for the level of work and discipline expected of them. He believed that the curriculum and rules of conduct should be modified to hold cadets to a higher standard. And though the course schedule was crowded, Lee thought it left out important subjects.

It also troubled Colonel Lee that the administrative chain of command ignored rules and procedures, which made it hard to maintain discipline. When boys were dismissed for failing academically or violating standards of conduct, their parents or sponsors appealed to Secretary of War Conrad, who often ordered their reinstatement. Fortunately for the colonel, the presidential election of 1852 would bring a change in administration, a new secretary of war, and a new attitude. Lee's former commander and champion, General Winfield Scott, was the Whig Party candidate opposing his former brigadier, Franklin Pierce, now a New Hampshire senator and legislator. Scott was defeated, but Pierce installed a new secretary of war far more in line with Lee's thinking when it came to upholding standards and rejecting political pressure.

Conrad's replacement was Jefferson Davis, previously a

senator from Mississippi, who had graduated from West Point one year ahead of Lee in 1828. Davis and Lee had much in common, though it would be years before the power of their bond was evident. Davis left a promising career in the army in 1835 to marry the daughter of then Colonel Zachary Taylor, who opposed the match. Three months after the wedding, Davis and his bride, Sarah, both came down with malaria, and Sarah died. In 1845 he was elected to the U.S. House of Representatives, and he married Varina Howell, granddaughter of New Jersey Governor Richard Howell. He resigned from the House a year later to raise a regiment of Mississippi volunteers for the war in Mexico. Wounded during the Battle of Buena Vista, he was offered a general's commission by President James K. Polk. Davis declined the honor, saying the president had no authority to grant a commission in a Mississippi state regiment. That right was properly reserved for the state.

In the fall of 1852, Colonel and Mrs. Lee and two of their children moved to West Point, along with their dogs, cats, horses, and household slaves. The superintendent's house was a large, comfortable two-story stone residence on the grounds with a decorative wrought iron fence around it and a stable in back. Mary loved the garden with a pond and greenhouse behind the house, and she promptly set out plant cuttings from Arlington. Custis, starting his second year as a cadet, would remain at the barracks. Rooney and Daughter were away at separate boarding schools, and Annie and Agnes had stayed with their tutor at Arlington, leaving only Rob and Mildred to enroll at the school for officers' children on the post.

The first academic term of 1853 began on a promising note. Lee had excellent support from the War Department and the new president, discipline and regulations were tightened, and his son had dramatically improved his performance in his second year after a shaky start. One note of sadness came from a telegram Mrs. Lee received from her father on April 24 warning that her mother was gravely ill. Mary left by train immediately, traveling day and night to reach home before breakfast on the twenty-sixth, but she was too late. Mrs. Custis had complained of a headache on the twenty-first that rapidly got worse. Awakened by the late night activity on the twenty-third, Annie and Agnes, crying and afraid, stood in the doorway of their grandmother's room. She motioned them to climb into bed with her and asked, "How can you cry so?" Softly she recited the Lord's Prayer, closed her eyes, and stopped breathing.

Colonel Lee felt he couldn't leave his duties, and with Mr. Custis incapacitated by grief, Mary handled all the funeral arrangements. On June 21 she greeted President and Mrs. Pierce when they came to Arlington for a condolence call. Robert wrote to encourage her and remind her of God's providence:

> May God give you the strength to enable you to bear and say, "His will be done." She has gone from all trouble, care and sorrow to a holy immortality, there to rejoice and praise forever the God and Savior she so long and truly served. Let that be our comfort and that our consolation. May our death be like hers, and may we meet in happiness in Heaven.

## TEN

# Doctrines and Miracles

THE SUMMER AFTER Mrs. Custis died, Mary talked with her daughters Mary and Annie about being confirmed in the church. The three of them felt it was an important, life-changing step, and they discussed it in detail so the girls' hearts would be properly prepared. Mary was overjoyed when Robert decided to be confirmed as well. It was Sunday, July 17, 1853, that the family went to Christ Church in Alexandria and the Episcopal bishop of Virginia, John Johns, delivered a sermon based on John 6:68: "Then Simon Peter answered him, Lord, to whom shall we go? thou hast the words of eternal life." This was a direct and unwavering call to follow Christ. When the moment came, Robert, Mary, and Annie knelt at the chancel rail together to take their first Communion.

Mary left a detailed, intimate record of her spiritual journey in her prayer journal. Nothing like it exists for Robert. In an age when men seldom showed or expressed their emotions, Lee was far more expressive than most. He wrote freely of his love for his wife and children. He cared deeply for the cadets under his command at West Point, setting aside an hour for them in his office every morning from seven until eight o'clock, keeping an eye on any who were struggling, and writing to parents to prod or encourage those who needed it. Yet up to this time he seldom wrote of or discussed his personal religious beliefs.

Historians are divided over the impact of Lee's confirmation on him and what it meant. Douglas Southall Freeman, Pulitzer Prize-winning author of a four-volume biography of Lee, commented,

> In early boyhood [Lee] had been drilled in his catechism by Reverend William Meade. From his youth he lived in the spiritual atmosphere Meade had created in northern Virginia, but he had not joined any church. As he grew older all his religious impulses were deepened, and he felt an increasing dependence on the mercy of a personal God. It is probable that the Mexican War, the death of Mrs. Custis, and his sense of responsibility for so many young men brought the great questions of faith closer to him. More particularly, as both Mary and Annie were now of age to be confirmed, Lee decided that he ought also to submit himself formally to the Christian faith.

Writing thirty years after Freeman, Lee biographer Clifford Dowdey took the same evidence to a far different conclusion.

This act [of being confirmed] has been grossly misunderstood, even confused with some religious emotionality leading him to "join the church." Lee had always thought of himself as belonging to the church, as shown by serving on the vestry at Fort Hamilton.

. . . when he was growing up, young confirmations were not common practice in Virginia. This was a vestige of Colonial days when the Church of England did not maintain bishops in the colony. Since only bishops performed the "laying on of hands," the communicants came to regard confirmation as unimportant. . . . Lee had been baptized as a child and had learned the Catechism (which actually prepared him to receive confirmation) from Reverend William Meade, later bishop, when he was rector at Christ Church.

When Lee's children were growing, the old custom began to change. Then it happened that on a family visit to Arlington, Agnes [sic] and Annie were confirmed at Christ Church, and it occurred either to Lee or his wife that he had never performed this ceremony. As a bishop was available, he joined his daughters at the chancel. . . . Nothing was changed for Lee, but perhaps his children felt better about him as a fellow communicant.

It's hard to imagine "nothing was changed" in a man whose feelings ran as deep as Lee's did. As he got older, Lee referred to faith more often and seemed to feel it far more passionately. This could have been the consequence of age, the accumulated wisdom and life experience, that made him appreciate his faith more. It may be that Colonel Lee was also affected by his military service in Mexico and by Mrs. Custis's death. The more daunting the world appears, the more appealing the refuge of an all-powerful God can be.

After a visit to West Point, Secretary of War Davis wrote of Lee, "I was surprised to see so many gray hairs on his head . . . he confessed that the cadets did exceedingly worry him, and then it was perceptible that his sympathy with the young people was rather an impediment than a qualification for the superintendency."

It seems that Lee impressed everyone he knew. Of those West Point years, the colonel's son Rob recalled,

> My father was the most punctual man I ever knew. He was always ready for family prayers, for meals, and met every engagement, social or business, at the moment. He expected all of us to be the same. . . . I never knew him late for Sunday service at the Post Chapel. He used to appear some minutes before the rest of us, in uniform, jokingly rallying my mother for being late, and for forgetting something at the last moment. When he could wait no longer for her, he would say that he was off and would march along to church by himself, or with any of the children who were ready.

In their report after the graduation of 1854, the board of visitors of the academy declared about Lee:

> The board cannot conclude this report without bearing testimony to the eminent qualifications of the superintendent for

the honorable and distinguished post assigned him by the government. Services conspicuous in the field, and when our country was engaged in a war with a foreign nation, have lost none of their luster in the exalted position he so worthily fulfills.

Despite these glowing reports of his success as an educator, Lee soon faced the prospect of a new assignment as different from running a military academy as he could imagine. The army wanted him in the cavalry.

The president had authorized two new regiments of infantry and two of cavalry to protect soldiers and settlers in the West from attack by Indians. On March 3, 1855, Colonel Albert Sidney Johnston was appointed commander of the Second Cavalry in Texas and Lee was assigned as his lieutenant colonel. Accepting the new post meant a transfer from staff officer to an officer of the line, and from engineers to the cavalry. It would also mean a promotion to lieutenant colonel after seventeen years as a captain, though he'd have no pay increase since he was already drawing his brevet salary. "Promotion, if offered an officer, ought in my opinion to be accepted," Lee believed, "but it need not be sought unless deserved." Further advancement was more likely for Lee in the cavalry, where officers who outranked him were older and closer to retirement than in the Corps of Engineers.

True to form, Lee didn't let his personal or family needs stand in the way of duty. As he wrote to his frequent correspondent, Mary's cousin Markie Williams, "The change from my present confined and sedentary life, to one more free and active, will certainly be more agreeable to my feelings and serviceable to my health. But my happiness can never be advanced by my sepa-ration from my wife, children, and friends."

Colonel Johnston wasn't yet ready to assume his post. Therefore on April 20, 1855, Lee took direct command of troops for the first time in his military career. The Second Cavalry would be mustered in Louisville, Kentucky, so once again he left his wife and children in order to serve his country. Lee's rare ability to bal-ance discipline and obedience with insight and compassion was soon displayed, as described in a letter to his wife on July 1, while waiting for uniforms he'd requisitioned two months earlier:

> Yesterday, at muster, I found one of the [new recruits] in a dirty, tattered shirt and pants, with a white hat and shoes, with other garments to match. I asked him why he did not put on clean clothes. He said he had none. I asked him if he could not wash and mend those. He said he had nothing else to put on. I then told him immediately after muster to go down to the river, wash his clothes, and sit on the bank and watch the passing steamboats til they dried, and then mend them. This morn-ing at inspection he looked as proud as possible, stood in the position of a soldier with his little fingers on the seams of his pants, the beaver cocked back, and his toes sticking through his shoes, but his skin and solitary two garments clean. He grinned very happily at my compliments.

He missed his family terribly, but he wrote to Mary of his deeply rooted faith that all would be well. The question of whether it was there all along, or nurtured and encouraged by his confirmation, or stirred up by the thought of another long separation is less important than the proof that by now Lee was a sincerely and deeply religious man. He said,

> I am content to read my Bible & prayers alone & draw much comfort from their holy precepts & merciful promises, though I feel unable to follow one, & utterly unworthy of the other. I must still pray to that glorious God, without whom there is no help, & with whom there is no danger. That He may guard & protect you all, and more than supply you in my absence, is my daily & constant prayer.

Lee sailed for Galveston, Texas, on February 12, 1856, and arrived in San Antonio on March 6. For the next nineteen months, beginning April 9, he commanded two squadrons at Camp Cooper, using his ample spare time to pick a site for a fort in the area. When he arrived, there was not a single finished building, so Lee lived in a tent with daytime temperatures over a hundred degrees "like the blast from a hot-air furnace," water scarce and brackish, and plenty of tarantulas for company. His few egg-laying hens lived in a pen off the ground to keep snakes away.

Letters back and forth to Arlington continued in a steady stream. Along with family news and expressions of love, Robert and Mary wrote on two other topics more than before. One was business and money matters. Mary was largely managing the Arlington estate, and she also monitored the colonel's financial affairs. On her own she'd invested some of their money in railroad bonds. The other topic was Mary's delicate health. She'd developed painful stiffness in her joints, which she hoped a visit to a resort spring would help. When she wrote asking Robert how she should pay for the trip, he answered, "At this distance I can do nothing for you. You must make your own arrangements and carry out your own plans. I am at a loss however to know where you will get funds for your journey, as it seemed from your letter that you have deprived yourself of those you had in your possession before you knew how you could replace them."

The truth was that Mary's health was in serious decline. Though she didn't dwell on it or reveal its seriousness, she did tell the colonel something about her condition:

> My visit to the Springs only served to bring out & diffuse the disease. . . . [B]ut my progress has been slow & [the doctor] advises me to ride and walk about. The riding is very pleasant & does not tire me, but I walk very unsteadily & not often without a crutch. My general health is perfectly good, nor do I suffer much pain except when I move suddenly. I trust in my next letter I may be able to give you more cheering accounts.

He was at Fort Brown, near the mouth of the Rio Grande at the Gulf of Mexico, during Christmas 1856. Hearing of James Buchanan's election as president, he wrote to his wife, "I hope he will be able to extinguish fanaticism North and South, cultivate love for the country and Union, and restore harmony between the different sections."

Colonel Lee had reason to be worried. As both a federal army officer with a strong sense of duty and a Virginian with a deep respect for states' rights, Lee had watched with concern as the states' rights/slavery argument rose and fell and rose again. The Missouri Compromise of 1820 and the follow-up Compromise of 1850 had somewhat defused the issue of slavery on a national level and softened the war of words and occasional violence that marked the debate. Then in 1854 a new law, known as the Kansas-Nebraska Act, nullified the Missouri Compromise by allowing new territories in the West to decide on their own whether to permit slavery. When Kansas Territory applied for admission to the Union as a slave state, the House of Representatives rejected it. If the federal government could keep a state out of the Union for allowing slavery, could it reject other states that were already in for the same reason? Could Congress trump a state constitution, especially in South Carolina, Virginia, and other places where the institution of slavery predated the United States? This, it seemed, was another dangerous step toward splitting the country in two.

On December 27, 1856, Colonel Lee wrote to his wife again from Fort Brown. It was the clearest and most complete expression of his views on slavery ever recorded. Any question over whether Lee left the army years later over slavery or states' rights is unequivocally answered here. Lee thought that slavery was wrong and that it should be abolished. He never would have fought to defend slavery because he was unalterably opposed to it. On the other hand, he considered states' rights essential and inviolable:

> In this enlightened age, there are few I believe, but what will acknowledge, that slavery as an institution, is a moral & political evil in any Country. It is useless to expatiate on its

disadvantages. I think it however a greater evil to the white man than to the black race, & while my feelings are strongly enlisted in behalf of the latter, my sympathies are more strong for the former. The blacks are immeasurably better off here than in Africa, morally, socially & physically. The painful discipline they are undergoing, is necessary for their instruction as a race, & I hope will prepare & lead them to better things. How long their subjugation may be necessary is known & ordered by a wise Merciful Providence. Their emancipation will sooner result from the mild and melting influence of Christianity, than the storms & tempests of fiery Controversy. This influence though slow, is sure. The doctrines & miracles of our Saviour have required nearly two thousand years, to Convert but a small part of the human race, & even among Christian nations, what gross errors still exist! While we see the Course of the final abolition of human Slavery is onward, & we give it the aid of our prayers & all justifiable means in our power, we must leave the progress as well as the result in his hands who sees the end; who Chooses to work by slow influences; & with whom two thousand years are but as a Single day. Although the Abolitionist must know this, & must See that he has neither the right or power of operating except by moral means & suasion, & if he means well to the slave, he must not Create angry feelings in the Master; that although he may not approve the mode by which it pleases Providence to accomplish its purposes, the result will nevertheless be the same; that the reasons he gives for interference in what he has no Concern, holds good for every kind of interference with our neighbours when we disapprove their Conduct; Still I fear he will persevere in his evil Course. Is it not strange that the descendants of those pilgrim fathers who Crossed the Atlantic to preserve their own freedom of opinion, have always proved themselves intolerant of the Spiritual liberty of others?

God would sort out the question of slavery if only America had the patience to wait for Him. God was in control there and everywhere, even in the heartbreaking death of a child. One of Lee's sad duties as a commander was to conduct funeral services. His account of a ceremony for the infant son of a sergeant reinforces the image of his tenderness, his love for children, and his unflinching confidence that what God ordained was always right:

The thermometer ranges above one hundred degrees, but the sickness among the men is on the decrease, though there has been another death among the children. He was as handsome a little boy as I ever saw—the son of one of our sergeants, about a year old; I was admiring his appearance the day before he was taken ill. Last Thursday his little waxen form was committed to the earth. His father came to see me, the tears flowing down his cheeks, and asked me to read the funeral service over his body, which I did at the grave for the second time in my life. I hope I shall not be called on again, for, though I believe that it is far better for a child to be called by its heavenly Creator into his presence in its purity and innocence, unpolluted by sin, and uncontaminated by the vices of the world, still it so wrings a parent's heart with anguish that it is painful to see. Yet I know it was done in mercy to both—mercy to the child, mercy to the parents. The former has been saved from sin and misery here, and the latter have been given a touching appeal and powerful inducement to prepare for the hereafter. May it prove effectual, and may they require no further severe admonition!

From facing the sadness of death in Texas, Colonel Lee was called to deal with loss in his own family circle. Mary's father died on October 10, 1857, but Lee did not learn about it until eleven days later. He immediately requested a two-month leave of absence to help Mary settle Arlington's affairs. There was very little for a cavalry officer to do in Texas, and though Lee told his wife she was on her own in decision making, when a true crisis came, he put his family's needs ahead of pointless patrolling in the Texas scrub country. During his whole time in the Second Cavalry, the colonel never saw a single Indian.

Lee arrived at Arlington on November 11. His first surprise was to see how sick Mary actually was. She had been bedridden for weeks at a time and was in constant pain. Nevertheless, she handled the details of her father's funeral. The old master was buried in the garden next to his wife. His grave marker eventually would be a miniature Washington Monument, a copy of the still-unfinished honor to his foster grandfather that Custis had so championed and that he could see from his front porch.

The will, written in 1855, made Colonel Lee one of four executors, but Lee ultimately did all the work. Mr. Custis had died owning three plantations. Mrs. Lee received a life interest in Arlington, which would go to her son Custis after her death.

The White House, a plantation of four thousand acres in New Kent County, went to Rooney. This estate was part of Martha Washington's property by her first husband, John Parke Custis. Mr. Custis insisted that George and Martha Washington were married on the estate, though some accounts disputed his claim. Romancoke, also about four thousand acres and another Custis legacy in King William County, went to Rob. Colonel Lee received a lot in Washington, and each of the four granddaughters was to get $10,000, with other land sold to raise the money. Mr. Custis's will further directed that all Arlington slaves be emancipated within five years of his death.

A quick survey revealed almost $10,000 in debts but no cash. How to pay down the debt, raise $40,000 for the granddaughters, and free the slaves in five years was a daunting task for Lee to consider. It would be far longer than a two-month process. Lee had his leave extended to December 1, 1858, another full year. But as time approached for him to return to Texas, he asked for and received an extension to May 1, 1859, then yet another extension to September 1.

Aunt Maria Fitzhugh sent Lee $1,000 to help with short-term expenses, and dutiful Custis sent his father the deed to Arlington. Colonel Lee returned both. Lee spent some time at the White House Plantation getting it ready for Rooney and his new wife, Charlotte, to move into. They were married in March at Shirley Plantation, in the same room where Lee's mother and Light Horse Harry exchanged their vows.

Lee also addressed the problem of what to do with the slaves. Custis had given them very little to do, and they'd gotten used to days of light work or none at all. Lee introduced something more akin to military efficiency and precision, finding jobs on the plantation for some of them, and hiring out others, hoping to generate some of the $40,000 that his father-in-law had promised the Lee daughters before the slaves received their freedom.

Lee saw to the repair of buildings at all three estates, leased out the weed-choked mill at Arlington to a neighbor who knew that trade, sold the livestock, rebuilt roads and fences, rented some land to small farmers, and planted the rest in corn and wheat. By the fall of 1859, White House and Romancoke were turning a profit, and Arlington was breaking even.

During his long leave, Lee served on courts-martial and saw his professional reputation continue to grow. There was talk of a promotion to brigadier and speculation that Lee might be tapped to replace General Scott, now in his seventies, as general of the army.

In October 1859, General Scott offered him the position of military secretary. The high honor underscored the general's deep appreciation for Lee's abilities. But since the colonel had gone from staff to line, he didn't want to go back. Scott had expected that answer and respected it.

It was shortly after coming home from a court-martial in New York, on the morning of the seventeenth, that Lee was sitting at his desk when Jeb Stuart came riding up the drive. The sealed note he carried from Secretary of War John B. Floyd ordered Lee to Harpers Ferry.

## ELEVEN

# The Destiny of His State

COLONEL LEE EXPECTED to return to Texas once he declined General Scott's offer to stay in Washington. He secured an assignment in the District for his son Custis so he could watch over Arlington and their increasingly disabled wife and mother. After more than two years away from the cavalry, Lee finally left for Texas on February 10, 1860, assigned to temporary command of the Department of Texas. As there was no colonel in the department, he would be the highest-ranking officer.

Lee arrived at department headquarters in San Antonio on February 19 and took command the next day. As before, there was very little to do in the isolated outpost. Lee was supposed to go on the offensive against the Indians who were scalping and terrorizing settlers farther west, but would have to wait until later in the season when there would be enough prairie grass for the horses.

Eighteen sixty was an election year, and that May the Republican Party nominated Abraham Lincoln as its first national candidate. The party platform stated that slavery would not be allowed to spread beyond states where it was already legal, which would negate the Kansas-Nebraska Act, which had in turn undone the Missouri Compromise. The Republicans also said they would call for protective tariffs that Southerners believed would help Northern manufacturers but hurt Southern interests. The Democrats were in disarray. After fifty-seven nominating ballots during their April convention in Charleston, South Carolina, they adjourned without a candidate. At a second convention in Baltimore two months later, they finally chose Stephen Douglas, Lincoln's former debating partner.

On November 6, Lincoln won with less than 40 percent of the vote in a four-way race, which also included John C. Breckinridge of Kentucky as a second Democratic candidate and John Bell of Tennessee representing the Constitutional Union Party. Four days later, South Carolina issued a call to secede. By the end of January 1861, five other states—Mississippi, Florida, Alabama, Georgia, and Louisiana—had joined the South Carolinians, and Texans were leaning in the same direction. Texas governor Sam Houston (Mrs. Lee's one-time beau) opposed secession, but on February 1, a special convention of the state legislature passed an ordinance of secession 166 to 7. General Winfield Scott was one of numerous prominent Americans who believed the United States should allow states to secede. Newspaperman Horace

Greeley agreed, writing in the *New York Tribune*, "We hope never to live in a republic whereof one section is pinned to the residue by bayonets."

The Confederate States of America adopted a provisional constitution on February 7 and appointed Jefferson Davis as president. Though events were gathering momentum, the state of Virginia voted on February 4 not to secede by a margin of two to one. The same day, Virginia staged a peace conference in Washington to try and defuse the crisis. Mary Lee knew her husband's heart, and to a friend she later wrote, "From the first commencement of our troubles he had decided that in the event of Virginia's secession, duty . . . would compel him to follow."

With Texas leaving the Union, General Scott summoned Lee to Washington. There the two Virginians had a three-hour private meeting. Erasmus D. Keyes, Scott's military secretary, didn't think that Scott expected Lee to fight against the South, but perhaps Lee could help the United States make a preemptive move that would prevent war altogether. The colonel could command an army so overwhelmingly powerful that the Confederacy would rather back down than fight. On March 16, 1861, President Lincoln had signed Lee's commission as a full colonel, and Lee received it on March 28.

Between the day Lincoln approved Lee's commission and the day Lee got it, the colonel probably received a letter written March 15 by L. P. Walker, the Confederate secretary of war, offering Lee a commission as a brigadier general in the Confederate army. If Lee sent an answer, no record of it remains.

To that point, the Confederacy had not supported its claim

of independence with military action. That changed on April 12 when the breakaway government shelled Fort Sumter, South Carolina, a federal installation on an island in Charleston Harbor. Representatives of the Confederate States had offered to buy federal properties within their borders and sign a peace treaty. President Lincoln refused, saying their government wasn't legitimate and therefore they had no right to negotiate. South Carolina then demanded that the U.S. withdraw from Sumter. There the matter stood for a while. Neither side wanted to fire the first shot because neither wanted to be labeled as the aggressor.

The situation shifted when the Confederates learned that soldiers at the fort were running low on food and decided to attack before the men could be resupplied. Southern troops began shelling before dawn on April 12. The fort surrendered on the afternoon of April 13 and was evacuated on the fourteenth. No one on either side was killed in action, and the Confederates gave soldiers and families quartered at Sumter safe passage to Union territory.

The day after Fort Sumter fell, President Lincoln issued a proclamation calling for 75,000 soldiers to suppress the uprising and offered the rebellious states twenty days to put down their arms. On April 17, Lee received a message from General Scott asking him to see him the next day. The message was in a note from Francis Preston Blair, former editor of the *Congressional Globe*, requesting that Lee call on him the next day as well.

Blair had suggested to the president that Robert E. Lee head the huge new volunteer army, and Lincoln had authorized him to "ascertain Lee's intentions and feelings." Blair also discussed the matter with Secretary of War Simon Cameron, who told him to make the offer to Lee. The morning of April 18, Lee went to Blair's house, where Blair explained that a massive army of 75,000 to 100,000 men was being raised to enforce federal law. On the president's behalf, Blair invited Lee to command the new force as a major general.

Probably Lee had some idea of what Blair would offer, though the size of the force and the offer to skip over brigadier and go straight to major general must have impressed him. But Lee had long since made up his mind. He told Blair, "If the Union is dissolved and the government disrupted, I shall return to my native state and share the miseries of my people and save in defence will draw my sword on no one." In his own account of the meeting with Blair, Lee wrote, "I declined the offer he made me to take command of the army that was to be brought into the field, stating as candidly and as courteously as I could, that though opposed to secession and deprecating war, I could take no part in an invasion of the Southern States."

After his visit with Blair, Lee went to General Scott's office to break the news. "Lee," the general supposedly said, "you have made the greatest mistake of your life; but I feared it would be so."

Lee's wife shared his fear of disaster should the Union fall apart. To a friend, she wrote,

Only God can stay the waves of anarchy & disunion & make the passions of men subservient to His will. We of the South have had great provocation, yet for my part I would rather endure the ills we know than rush madly into greater evils—& what could be greater than the division of our glorious Republic into petty states, each seeking its private interests & unmindful of the whole.

On April 19, Virginia seceded from the United States but didn't join the Confederacy. Hearing the news, Lee remarked, "I must say that I am one of those dull creatures that cannot see the good of secession." That afternoon Lee walked for a long time in the rose garden at Arlington and paced around the house. Friends had gathered to discuss secession, but early in the evening Lee left his wife to entertain them and went up to his room. For hours, until all the guests were gone, Mary heard her husband pacing upstairs, dropping several times to his knees in prayer. She waited patiently downstairs until, long after midnight, he came down holding two letters. The first read,

Arlington, Virginia (Washington City P.O.)

20 April 1861

Hon. Simon Cameron

Secty of War

Sir:

I have the honor to tender the resignation of my commission as Colonel of the 1st Regt. of Cavalry.

Very resp'y Your Obedient Servant.

R. E. Lee

Col 1st Cav'y.

The other was a long letter to General Scott, the friend and mentor who meant so much to him, explaining his decision to the man who, after the Mexican War, had called Lee "not only the greatest living soldier of America, but the greatest now living in the world." As quickly as Lee acted, his sense of honor prompted him to admit that he could have moved faster. His resignation "would have been presented at once," he explained, "but for the struggle it has cost me to separate myself from a service to which I have devoted the best years of my life, and all the ability I possessed. . . . Save in defense of my native state, I never desire to again draw my sword."

"My husband has wept tears of blood over this terrible war," Mary observed, "but as a man of honor and a Virginian, he must follow the destiny of his state."

That evening Lee got a letter from John Robertson of Richmond, former congressman and a member of the unsuccessful peace committee, asking the colonel to meet him. Robert left Alexandria for Richmond by train the morning of April 22. He would never see Arlington again.

Word spread that Lee was conferring with Virginia leaders. Whenever the train stopped along the way that day, the colonel felt obliged to step onto the back of the rear car and acknowledge the cheers of the crowds. At the state capitol in Richmond, Lee learned that the state convention of April 19 authorized the state to appoint a commander of military and naval forces in Virginia "with the rank of major general and authority to direct the organization and operations of the troops under the governor's constitutional control." Governor John Letcher had formally offered Lee the position on April 21 and sent a messenger, whom Lee probably passed on the way. Robert accepted command of the state militia, declaring once again that he would draw his sword only in his state's defense.

The evening of his first day as a general, Lee had a visit from Alexander Stephens, former Georgia congressman and now vice president of the Confederate States. He requested a military alliance between Virginia and the Confederacy. If that happened, he explained, Lee might find himself answering to a general of lesser grade since brigadier was the highest rank in the Southern army at the time. According to Stephens, Lee

> expressed himself as perfectly satisfied, and as being very desirous to have the alliance formed. He stated, in words which produced thorough conviction in my mind of their perfect sincerity, that he did not wish anything connected with himself individually, or his official rank or *personal* position, to interfere in the slightest degree with the immediate consummation of that measure which he regarded as one of the utmost importance in every possible view of public considerations.

The Northern newspapers pounded Lee mercilessly. They heaped scorn on all the officers and politicians who went over to the Confederate side, but seemed to save an extra measure of venom for Colonel Lee because of his high profile and his historic family connections. One essay criticizing the "ingrates and traitors" of the South made special mention of his heritage:

Lee once professed to greatly venerate the memory and example of the great Washington. He even married the daughter of George Washington Parke Custis . . . [who] never tired of writing and eloquently portraying the virtues and eminent deeds of the Father of his Country. . . . [If Custis] could have lived until now, he would have good cause to be bowed down in grief and sorrow to behold his son-in-law following in the footsteps of Benedict Arnold.

If Lee saw the article and others like it, he had little time to fret over them. From his headquarters at the Spotswood Hotel in Richmond over the next few weeks, he oversaw a whirlwind of activity. On May 10, still a major general in the Virginia state militia, Lee received an order from the War Department of the Confederacy authorizing him to "assume control of the forces of the Confederate States in Virginia, and assign them to such duties as you may indicate, until further orders." Four days later he accepted a commission as a brigadier general in the army of the Confederate States of America. On May 23, Virginia publicly ratified the ordinance of secession.

President Lincoln's peace offer had expired on May 5. Since Virginia had already committed acts of war against the United States, the state had to be ready for an invasion. That meant that General Robert E. Lee, CSA, had to fabricate a national military command out of nothing while sitting at a desk in a Richmond hotel room. There was no staff, no strategic military plan, no chain of command, no coordinated system of enlistment or conscription, no supply lines, uniforms, tents, flags, or anything else, and no money to pay for it. In the weeks ahead, Lee would have to depend on his engineer's eye for systems, precision, and detail; his incredible personal stamina; and his inspirational effect on everyone who served under him. He was responsible for knitting a loose confederation of state militias, volunteers, ex-U.S. Army soldiers, and others into a viable military force.

With about a million white residents and half that many black, almost all of them slaves, Virginia was the most populous state in the South and an obvious source of leadership for the Southern cause. Virginia was rich in cropland and home to important seaports. But from the first day, Lee struggled to field and equip an army to fight against an opponent with more of everything. The seceded states overall had far fewer people than the North, nine million against twenty-two million. The North in 1861 had ten times the industrial production of the South and more than thirty times the number of firearms.

One of Lee's first acts as a general in the Virginia militia was to secure the same arsenal at Harpers Ferry that he had recaptured for the United States against John Brown two years earlier. Virginia citizens stormed the arsenal on April 18 to claim its rifles and other supplies. Before they could break in, the U.S. commander set fire to the buildings and destroyed a reported sixteen thousand rifles. However, valuable weapons manufacturing machinery survived the blaze, and Lee's plan was to move it to Richmond where defenses were better.

Lee sent Major Thomas J. Jackson to command operations at Harpers Ferry and move the machinery. The two men probably hadn't seen each other since Mexico, until Jackson came to ask about the possibility of enlisting students from Virginia Military Institute in Lexington, where Jackson was a professor. In a sign of the confusion of the moment, the Confederate government sent Joseph E. Johnston to take command at Harpers Ferry, either ignoring Lee's decision or unaware of it. Jackson arrived to find two thousand volunteers and militiamen already there, ready for action but woefully unorganized. He drilled the men and traced weapons from the arsenal that might be recovered.

Meanwhile the Arlington mansion, one of the most familiar and prominent landmarks in the area, still stood in bold relief on the Virginia bluff just across the Potomac from Washington. Until 1846 the estate had been part of the District of Columbia. That year, the government gave the portion of what had been a perfect square lying on the Virginia side of the river back to the state. That meant that Arlington was in enemy territory, located on strategic high ground overlooking the capital. A Northern newspaper described it as "a nest of traitors" and a likely spot for the rebels to launch an invasion.

While General Lee continued with his planning in Richmond, his wife did her best to carry on as normally as possible. Driving through the District one day, she saw a New York regiment parading into town, trying its best to put on an impressive display, but garnering scarcely any interest from the people on the street. "Not a cheer was raised even from a small boy," Mrs. Lee remembered later. As she was leaving town, a member of the regiment she had known at West Point came up to her carriage to say hello. She asked him what the men were doing.

The soldier answered, "We were summoned here to defend the

Capitol which we were told was in imminent danger & expected to see Jeff Davis with an army of at least 30,000 men on Arlington Heights." He pointed up at Mary's home.

Mrs. Lee, no doubt with a chuckle, replied, "Come over and judge for yourself. I will secure you against capture."

General Lee knew his wife's magnificent home was a prime target for capture by the Federals. Rumors like the one Mrs. Lee's friend had heard continued, and even if the Confederates had no intention of fortifying the Arlington lawn, the Federals would assume the worst. Besides, U.S. troops would want the spot for their own defensive artillery. On April 26 Lee wrote his wife from Richmond:

> I am very anxious about you. You have to move and go to some point of safety, which you must select. The Mount Vernon plate and pictures ought to be secured. Keep quiet while you remain and in your preparation. War is inevitable, and there is no telling when it will burst around you. Virginia, yesterday, I understand, joined the Confederate States. What policy they may adopt I cannot conjecture. May God bless and preserve you, and have mercy on all our people.

As tensions mounted, Robert continued sending letters of warning. April 30: "You had better prepare all things for removal, that is, plate, pictures, etc., and be prepared at any moment." May 2: "I want you to be in a place of safety. . . . We have only to be resigned to God's will and pleasure, and do all we can for our protection." Yet still Mary resisted. Spring was in full bloom at

Arlington, and other than some soldiers marching in the District, there was no sign of war. It seemed almost surreal to imagine leaving the only home she had ever known, even temporarily, when everything appeared so calm and peaceful.

Her perspective changed a few days later when a young Federal lieutenant named Orton Williams came up to her room where she was painting a portrait of her son Rob. Orton was a familiar face in the house, both as grandson of Mary's aunt Martha Custis Peter and as daughter Agnes's current beau.

"You've got to get out now," he told Mary. "Union troops are ready to take Arlington Heights."

Mrs. Lee didn't have to ask who sent him. Orton, newly commissioned, was on General Scott's staff. The kind and venerable Virginian, one of only a handful who had not resigned his U.S. commission, was secretly warning her that the invasion was coming and she should get out while she could. The next morning Orton came again to tell her the action had been temporarily delayed, but she should move as soon as possible.

Days later, Williams informed his superiors that he wished to resign his commission so he could join the Confederacy. They offered him a post as a cavalry instructor at West Point if he stayed. When he refused, he was arrested as a traitor who had supposedly sneaked to Arlington to reveal details of the Federal occupation plan. Mary wrote to her husband, "All his assurances that he considered himself bound in honor not to reveal anything & that you & I had advised him to remain in the U.S. service as long as he could & be of use to Genl. Scott were not credited."

Orton's warning spurred Mary to action at last as Robert's

urgent letters continued. May 11: "You had better complete your arrangements and retire further from the scene of war. It may burst upon you at any time. It is sad to think of the devastation, if not ruin, it may bring upon a spot so endeared to us. But God's will be done. We must be resigned." On May 13 he added,

> Make your plans for several years of war. If Virginia is invaded, which appears to be designed, the main routes through the country will, in all probability, be infested and passage interrupted. The times are indeed calamitous. The brightness of God's countenance seems turned away from us, and its mercy stopped in its blissful current. It may not always be so dark, and He may in time pardon our sins and take us under his protection.

Some of her children prepared to join her, while others followed their father into uniform. Custis and Rooney were commissioned in the Virginia army. Rob wanted to fight, too, but his parents thought the seventeen-year-old was too young. As Mary and her family pondered when they should leave, she noticed a dramatic increase in river traffic, and one day she saw two Confederate soldiers scouting her hillside on horseback. Slaves began sneaking away at night. She had the family silver, George Washington's personal papers, and the Custis and Lee family papers packed into two crates and sent by train to her husband in Richmond. Martha Washington's damask draperies went into the attic, and the Washington state china and other Mount Vernon treasures were crated and locked in the cellar.

Mary decided to go to Ravensworth for the time being. Isolated in the country, the huge 22,000-acre property would be relatively safe. On May 8, Mary sent a wagonload of food, clothes, wine, housekeeping supplies, and the family piano. Daughter and Agnes rode with the luggage, Rob and Mildred were away at school, Rooney was at White House Plantation with his wife and new baby, and Annie was visiting them there. Only Mary and a few household slaves remained, along with Custis, who would escort his mother to safety before joining his father in Richmond.

Mary never expected to be gone more than a few weeks at most. In one letter she referred to the evacuation as a "visit of about 10 days." Likely she anticipated a temporary occupation that would prove the Confederacy had no military plans for the Heights, and then she would get back home in time to welcome the spring flowers she so enjoyed. One morning in the middle of May, Mary handed the house keys—the symbol of her position as owner and hostess at Arlington—to Selina Gray, her trusted personal maid, whose mother had cared for G. W. P. Custis as a boy at Mount Vernon. Moving painfully on crutches because of her arthritis, Mary settled into her coach with Custis's help and said good-bye to the crying servants. Mary wept too.

For a week or so the plantation carried on its usual routine out of sheer momentum, its livestock tended, gardens worked, and furniture dusted. The commander of the Virginia militia in the area was ordered not to come near the house to avoid inciting the Federals. Even so, there were rumors that the Confederates were installing an artillery battery on the lawn. On the moonlit night of May 23, ten thousand Federal troops swept across the

Potomac bridges and set up camp on the grounds of the grand mansion of "ex-Colonel Lee."

Mary and her family would never spend another night at Arlington. In fact, for as long as she lived, Mary never spent another night under a roof of her own.

## TWELVE

# I Must Continue

OVER THE NEXT several weeks, Lee continued the Herculean task of organizing a national army. On June 8, 1861, the Virginia state militia was mobilized with 40,000 men and officially transferred to the Confederate States. It was August 31 before Lee was commissioned a full general in command of Confederate troops.

He had not asked for or even wanted the position. As Lee had written to Mary on June 9, "I do not know what my position will be. I should like to retire to private life, so that I could be with you and the children, but if I can be of service to the State or her cause, I must continue." Two days later he added, "In this time of great suffering of the State and the country, our private distresses we must bear with resignation, and not aggravate them by repining, trusting to a kind and merciful God to overrule them for our own good."

He would return endlessly to this theme over the next four terrifying years: God is in control, His will is always best, and our responsibility is to humble ourselves and submit to His way.

Virginia invited President Davis to move the capital from Montgomery, Alabama, to Richmond on April 27, and on May 21 he accepted. Politically it might have been a good move, since Virginia was the largest and wealthiest of the Confederate states and Richmond was the bigger and more cosmopolitan city. Strategically it was a serious mistake. Montgomery was securely protected in the middle of the new nation, its factories and stores far from enemy lines. Richmond was a seaport near the Northern border, vulnerable to attack and difficult to defend. As the capital, it suddenly took on symbolic importance all out of proportion to its practical value.

Besides organizing an army, the South had to figure out how to pay for it. As an agrarian society, the South had long lagged behind the North in trade, capital accumulation, and investment. Along with everything else it had to do, the new government desperately needed to set up a treasury, establish credit, print money, issue bonds, and convince foreign governments to trade with it. Lee knew that fighting was inevitable. But the country had to be ready first. There seemed to be a public sense that all the South had to do was trot out and overrun the Federals, and that would be the end of it.

Lee delayed any general mobilization of his still-forming army until after Lincoln's May 5 deadline. He had no systems in place to train, equip, or transport soldiers and no way to supply them in the field. They also needed firearms. When Virginia handed its militia over to the Confederacy, the troops had 46,000 rifles in all. By comparison, in 1861 the Union army issued almost 1.3 million firearms to its soldiers.

On May 28, Lee left Richmond to inspect the troops at Manassas, an important railroad junction on a tributary of the Potomac called Bull Run. There was already a large force defending the railroad, camped about twenty-five miles from Washington, and the general drew up a plan of defense and counterattack for the invasion he knew was coming. Manassas was on the road between Washington and Richmond, and the Union military was under enormous public pressure to take Richmond and bring this nascent rebellion to a halt.

The Union army, led by General Irvin McDowell, was as unprepared for war as the Confederates, with volunteers just beginning to muster and only about 16,000 men available for duty. Lincoln pressed McDowell to attack the rebels and their capital before they could move on Washington. When McDowell insisted that he and his men weren't ready for combat, Lincoln argued that the rebels weren't ready either. Bowing to pressure and eager for a quick victory, McDowell finally set off against the Confederates on July 16.

With Lee back in Richmond, the Confederate army of about 23,000 men under General P. G. T. Beauregard had formed an effective defensive perimeter at Manassas. McDowell spent several days trying to outflank his outnumbered opponent, which gave 10,000 reinforcements under General Joseph E. Johnston time to arrive from the Shenandoah River Valley, where Union General Robert Patterson had tried unsuccessfully to keep them boxed in. McDowell's dearth of experience kept him from coordinating his forces to hold back Johnston's troops.

On the morning of July 21, McDowell sent his columns against the entrenched rebels, but their lack of field experience worked against them. One of the advancing columns marched in front of the troops sent to execute a flanking maneuver, blocking their path. Roads that the Union columns planned to use were too narrow. Finally, however, the attackers reached the junction, and after a morning of fighting, men commanded by Colonel William T. Sherman managed to ford Bull Run at an unguarded point and flank the Confederates. When the rebels fell back over a hill to regroup, McDowell failed to press his advantage and ordered an artillery bombardment instead.

Around midday, the shaken Confederates were reinforced by forces led by Colonels Wade Hampton and Thomas J. Jackson, and by cavalry under Colonel Jeb Stuart. Jackson positioned his men just behind the crest of a hill where they could fire their field-pieces and then reload them in safety on the downhill side. The rebel smoothbores hit their marks, while the Union's rifled artillery, designed for longer ranges, fired harmlessly over their heads. General Barnard Bee reported that Colonel Jackson stood "like a stone wall" against the Union advance, though later there was some question whether this was a compliment for holding his position or a complaint for not moving sooner to support a counterattack.

A key moment in the battle came when a Virginia unit moved to attack two Federal artillery guns at the end of the line being positioned to fire *en enfilade* against them, aiming along the line from one side rather than from the front. Confederate soldiers still wore whatever state militia uniforms they could scrounge, and the Virginia men were in blue that the Union commander mistook for his own men. By the time he realized his mistake, it was too late, and the guns were captured. Colonel Jackson pressed his men to keep up the attack, encouraging them to "yell like furies" as they charged, producing a bloodcurdling sound soon known as the rebel yell, a cross between a yodel, a scream, and an Indian war whoop.

By the middle of the afternoon, the Union was in retreat. More reinforcements from the Shenandoah Valley under Jubal Early and Kirby Smith added to the Southern momentum, and Beauregard ordered his whole command forward. The Union withdrawal became a rout. When an overturned wagon blocked a bridge, soldiers dropped their rifles and scurried back toward Washington in complete disorder. Hundreds of Federals were captured, though the rebels didn't press their advantage because they were struggling to communicate and coordinate their movements. A milling crowd of civilians added more confusion to the scene. Washington residents, excited at the spectacle and expecting a quick victory, had packed picnics and come out to watch the battle. Retreating soldiers ran headlong into families hustling back to town in their carriages. Washingtonians feared that Confederate troops would roll right into town, but they did not.

"We have won a glorious though dear-bought victory," Davis reported to Lee by telegram. "Night closed on the enemy in full flight and closely pursued." Lee's planning and preparation had enormous impact on the Confederate success, but since he wasn't in the field, Beauregard got the lion's share of the glory. Davis promoted the Louisianan to general that day.

The South suffered fewer than 2,000 casualties in all, but the North lost nearly 2,900 killed, wounded, or captured. While the South could celebrate in the short run, the results showed both sides that the war would not end quickly. A new wave of resentment against the rebels flooded the North, and humiliated by the loss, the Union acted quickly. The next day, July 22, Lincoln authorized an army of 500,000 men for three-year enlistments. Within a week the president replaced General McDowell with the more capable George B. McClellan.

As the war got under way, it was clear that western Virginia would resist cooperating with the rest of the state and with the Confederacy. Custom, family ties, business interests, and the shared history and commerce of the Ohio River gave this region more in common with its neighbor Pennsylvania than with the politicians and planters across the mountains to the east.

The town of Grafton was already lost to the Federals, along with Philippi fifteen miles to the south. Colonel R. S. Garnett had been commissioned a brigadier and sent to take command in hopes of turning the situation around. Garnett arrived to find his infantry in poor condition and asked Lee for reinforcements. On July 5 he reported that the situation had improved because the Union had occupied as much of western Virginia as it was likely to want and probably wouldn't fight for more.

General Lee answered,

> I do not think it probable that the enemy will confine himself
> to that portion of the northwest country which he now holds,
> but, if he can drive you back, will penetrate as far as Staunton.

Your object will be to prevent him, if possible, and to restrict his limits within the narrowest range, which, although outnumbered, it is hoped by skill and boldness you will accomplish.

In his communiqué, he characterized the battle at Manassas as "a glorious victory" that "has lightened the pressure upon our front amazingly." He continued: "Do not grieve for the brave dead. Sorrow for those they left behind, friends, relations, and families. The former are at rest, the latter must suffer. The battle will be repeated there in greater force. I hope God will again smile upon us, and strengthen our hearts and arms."

Mrs. Lee had moved from Ravensworth to Kinloch, a plantation one of her cousins owned forty miles from Manassas. She'd heard the gunfire of Bull Run from the front lawn there. Like so many others, Mary and the children were shocked by the first scenes of war as ambulances filled with wounded rolled by the house. The nearby estate of Blantyre had become a field hospital, and daughters Mary and Mildred volunteered to help the doctors. In spite of her arthritis, Mary started knitting the general socks and sending them with her letters.

On July 28 Lee left Richmond for the west to coordinate operations in the Kanawha Valley. He arrived in Staunton to find the Southerners already demoralized and on the defensive. Yet the general could find a glimmer of joy and hope even under these grim conditions. Busy as he was, he took a moment to write Mary that the countryside was "magnificent. The valleys so beautiful, the scenery so peaceful. What a glorious world Almighty God has given us. How thankless and ungrateful we are, and how we labour to mar his gifts."

After Garnett fell in battle, Lee dispatched General W. W.
Loring to take his place. Lee wanted to ensure the safety of the
Virginia Central Railroad, an essential transportation lifeline
in the region. The general had instructed Loring to assess the
situation and make his own plans. The problem was that in the
absence of specific orders, Loring had done nothing. To make
matters worse, two other commanders in the region, Henry Wise
and John Floyd, both former governors of Virginia, were long-
time political opponents who despised each other. General Floyd
outranked Colonel Wise—yet another bone of contention—and
both men disliked Loring. Because of all the personal animosity,
regiments were not organized, rations for the men and fodder for
the horses were in short supply, and the campsites were so filthy
and disease-ridden that Lee left and set up his tent elsewhere.

Lee didn't have the authority to order the men to get along
and do their work. He could have written to President Davis asking for that authority, which Davis surely would have granted, but
he never did. Instead he relied on what one historian called "tac-
tical persuasion," which for three jealous, vainglorious men was
completely inadequate. Two of the men were not professional
soldiers, and one, Wise, had no military experience whatsoever.
All his life, Lee had been the consummate gentleman who led
with a firm but gentle hand. In this case he needed desperately
to shake matters up, demanding discipline and action instead of
childish bickering. However, that was not the way Robert E. Lee
commanded. His courtly leadership technique would bear bitter
fruit later on.

Unable to prod his defective troika, Lee went on personal

reconnoitering trips, collected information from scouts, and devised a plan for a flanking and enveloping movement on the enemy. He prodded Loring into action at last, early on the morning of September 12. It had been raining for weeks, and the roads were bottomless rivers of mud. Loring's men were hungry and demoralized. When the time came to move out, unit commanders up and down the column found excuses for hanging back. Lee rode the line trying to rally the troops, but by noon he gave up.

Having missed the chance to defeat the Federals, Lee devised another plan to move west through the steep Kanawha Valley and shore up support for the Confederacy. Not only would it pain Lee to see his beloved Virginia split in two, but the west was important for its fertile cropland and the river terminal at Wheeling. Problems continued between Floyd and Wise, both because they griped at each other and refused to coordinate forces, and because their inexperience led to one mistake after another.

The solution to Lee's dilemma came in a dispatch to Wise from Secretary of War Judah P. Benjamin ordering him to turn his command over to General Floyd "and report yourself in person to the Adjutant-General in this city with the least delay." Finally President Davis acted to separate the two political foes, but he wasted precious time and opportunities getting it done.

With all the valley troops consolidated under Floyd and the distraction of personal friction gone at last, Lee found his expectations rising. When General Loring brought him nine thousand reinforcements, the prospects for success improved even more. Since food and other supplies were low and the terrain was rough and rocky, Lee chose to wait on the Union to attack. Finally on the night of October 5, sentries heard wagons and men on the move. Floyd's men braced for action the next day, but they discovered that the Federals had slipped away during the night.

Undeterred, Lee prepared to chase the Union troops through the valley. While an editorial acknowledged that Lee was "able and accomplished" and that rain and mud had made his work difficult, the writer insisted that "excess of caution or malignant chance has wrought, by mere delay, much of the mischief that was dreaded from defeat. The general, we doubt not, now feels the necessity of a more adventurous policy, and he is quite able, we hope, of adapting his plans to the exigency." Lee might have countered that this wasn't his direct command and therefore not his responsibility. Had he forcefully taken charge and implemented his plans, he could have offset much of the damage caused by Loring's inaction.

Lee did all he thought he had the authority to do. The very day that the Federals retreated, Lee issued orders to drive the Union out of the Kanawha Valley. Unfortunately, it was a straightforward movement beset with calamity. Troops were critically short of food and forage. The squalid conditions of their camp had made many men sick and unfit for duty. The weather in the mountains was bitterly cold. It looked like the Federals were about to attack the Virginia Central Railroad, which had to be defended at all costs. Furthermore the Richmond newspapers had gotten wind of Lee's plans and published them.

On October 20, Lee called a halt. General Floyd insisted that an advance would let them capture the whole Federal army, but Lee knew he didn't have the resources to hold his native state together, and that the chance to keep Virginia in one piece had all but run out. A convention had passed acts separating the western counties of Virginia from the rest of the state on August 29, though the legislature in Richmond considered them invalid. Lincoln, however, recognized this "restored government." On October 24 this convention voted to form a separate state of West Virginia, which formally joined the Union a year and a half later, on June 20, 1863.

Returning to Richmond on October 31,1861, Lee rode into a storm of criticism. He had lost the west, the commentators said, because he was too cautious, too slow to act, too timid. Newspaper editors called him "Granny Lee" and branded him one whose reputation depended on his lineage rather than his accomplishments.

Lee took the criticism hard, but saw it as part of the job. According to his military attaché Walter Taylor, the general said, "While it was very hard to bear, it was perhaps quite natural that such hasty conclusions should be announced, and that it was better not to attempt a justification or defense, but to go on steadily in the discharge of duty to the best of our ability, leaving all else to the calmer judgment of the future and to a kind Providence."

## THIRTEEN

# A Hard-Pressed Debtor

IN HIS INAUGURAL address on March 4, 1861, President Lincoln repeated himself from an earlier speech when he said, "I have no purpose directly or indirectly to interfere with the institution of slavery in the States where it exists; I believe I have no lawful right to do so." The Republican campaign platform, which he also read, supported his position:

> Resolved, that the maintenance inviolate of the rights of the States, and especially the right of each State to order and control its own domestic institutions according to its own judgment exclusively, is essential to that balance of power on which the perfection and endurance of our political fabric depend, and we denounce the lawless invasion by armed

forces of the soil of any State or territory, no matter under what
pretext, as the gravest of crimes.

And yet Lee and Davis, a former U.S. military officer and
a former U.S. secretary of war, were plotting to protect a breakaway nation from "invasion by armed forces" of the United States.
Davis wasted no time second-guessing Lee or fretting over West
Virginia. The day after Lee returned to Richmond, Confederate
Secretary of War Benjamin learned that Union ships were con-
verging on Port Royal Sound, South Carolina. Davis wanted to
organize the Southern coastal defenses under one command and,
to Lee's surprise, chose him for the assignment. Chastened by his
experience in the Kanawha Valley, where inefficient lines of command were a costly hindrance, Lee asked Davis to clarify that he
was completely in charge. Lee's appointment was not popular at
first. The governors of South Carolina and Georgia didn't want
Granny Lee commanding troops in their states, and Davis took
special care to smooth their ruffled feathers.

Lee arrived for his new assignment at Coosawhatchie, the
rail station closest to Port Royal, on November 6, 1861. A review
of the situation convinced him that the Union had overpowering strength on the water. Nothing he had could stop them.
His plan was to shift the battle to land, withdrawing inland to
a line along the hundred miles of the Charleston and Savannah
Railroad to protect this lifeline between the two ports. Lee executed orders to fortify Fort Pulaski, Savannah, and Charleston;
block waterways where the Federals might probe; and consolidate his troops at points on the railroad where the Union was
most likely to attack.

Most of the Lees gathered for Christmas that year at Rooney's White House Plantation. Though he would miss the modest family festivities, Robert looked forward to the season. "I shall think of you all on that holy day more intensely than usual," he wrote on December 2, "and shall pray to the great God of Heaven to shower His blessings upon you in this world, and to unite you all in His courts in the world to come. With a grateful heart I thank Him for His preservation thus far, and trust to His mercy and kindness for the future. Oh that I were more worthy, more thankful for all He has done and continues to do for me!"

On Christmas Day, Robert wrote several letters to his wife and children, reminiscing "with pleasure" about the grand Christmases at Arlington, but insisting that they shouldn't worry or regret their current circumstances: "Now we must be content with the many blessings we receive. If we can only become sensible to our transgressions, so as to be fully penitent and forgiven, that this heavy punishment under which we labour may with justice be removed from us and the whole nation, what a gracious consummation of all that we have endured it will be!"

He wrote of his fear that by now Arlington had been ruined by occupying troops. "You see what a poor sinner I am," he declared, "and how unworthy to possess what was given me; for that reason it has been taken away. I pray for a better spirit, and that the hearts of our enemies may be changed. In your homeless condition, I hope you make yourself contented and useful. Occupy yourself in aiding those more helpless than yourself."

It was a measure of the man that with so many cares upon his shoulders, he took the time to pick fresh wildflowers for one of the girls:

I send you some sweet violets, that I gathered for you this morning while covered with dense white frost, whose crystals glittered in the bright sun like diamonds, and formed a brooch of rare beauty and sweetness which could not be fabricated by the expenditure of a world of money. May God guard and preserve you for me, my dear daughter! Among the calamities of war, the hardest to bear, perhaps, is the separation of families and friends. Yet all must be endured to accomplish our independence, and maintain our self-government.

General Lee spent the first weeks of the new year of 1862 reinforcing his defensive line along the railroad and trying to recruit and arm more men. Confederate ships had to run blockades in order to deliver rifles and other supplies. Governors resisted turning militiamen over to Confederate control, and they disagreed about who was responsible for equipping the men and how long their enlistment should be. Lee dealt with these problems while making inspection tours up and down the coast. On the way to Florida in January, he stopped at Cumberland Island to visit his father's grave for the first time. Convinced that the Federals were focusing their attention on Savannah, he moved his headquarters there.

February brought a series of serious setbacks. On the sixth, the Federals, under a little-known general named U. S. Grant, captured Fort Henry on the Tennessee River. On the eighth, General Wise abandoned Roanoke Island, South Carolina. On the fifteenth, Union troops supported by gunboats on the Cumberland River captured fifteen thousand Confederates at Fort Donelson, east of

Nashville. Lee had to abandon any defense of Florida and send the soldiers from there to General Albert Sidney Johnston in Tennessee to hold onto crucial ground in the middle of the Confederacy.

The Confederate legislature was unhappy with the progress of the war and with President Davis's inclination to direct military operations on his own. The legislators wanted Davis to name a new secretary of war and expected Lee to be appointed. But Davis insisted that for all his admiration of Lee, a soldier should not be a cabinet secretary. This decision set off a political skirmish that ended with Lee being assigned "under the President [as commander in chief] with the conduct of military operations in the armies of the Confederacy."

The new position came with a long list of liabilities including political snarls, shortages of men and supplies, and the enemy closing in on several fronts. Again it was a job he didn't request and didn't want, but one he took because he felt it was his duty. In a letter to his family at White House he confided, "It will give me great pleasure to do anything I can to relieve [President Davis] and serve the country, but I cannot see either advantage or pleasure in my duties. But I will not complain, but do the best I can."

Reviewing the situation, he observed, "Our enemies are pressing everywhere, and our army is in the fermentation of organization. I pray that the great God may aid us, and am endeavoring by every means in my power to bring out the troops and hasten them to their destination." Lee believed the Federals would try to capture the Confederate capital. Somehow they had to hold onto enough troops to defend Richmond while answering non-stop appeals for reinforcements in other places. The Union was invading North Carolina, twenty steamboats full of soldiers were unloading at the southern tip of the Virginia Peninsula, Federals were stationed all along the Potomac for miles in both directions from Washington, and in the west other enemy columns pressed eastward from the new West Virginia.

As badly as the South needed soldiers, it needed weapons even more desperately. Lee had to send unarmed troops to General John B. Magruder at Yorktown and tell him to arm them with rifles from men in the hospitals. Some men received old-fashioned flintlocks until they too were all gone. Other troops fought with nothing but pikes. As Freeman noted, "Like a hard-pressed debtor, he had to borrow where he could to meet his most pressing obligations, trusting that, if his new creditors became troublesome, the future would bring the means with which to repay them."

Lee wanted to hold invaders as far down the Virginia Peninsula as he could, and he kept sending troops there at Magruder's request until his command of 11,000 had expanded to 53,000. Lee knew that thousands of one-year enlistments would be up soon, making matters even worse. He petitioned the governor of Virginia to draft all soldiers who didn't reenlist, and he hoped for the same action from other states. The Confederate Congress eventually passed a conscription bill. Unfortunately it was peppered with changes and exemptions, but at least it was a framework for action that gave Lee some hope that his army wouldn't simply dissolve.

In the West there was little good news. The Confederates claimed a victory at Shiloh, where General Grant was rumored to be drunk on duty. But General Johnston fell in the battle, and the rebels failed to keep Grant's Army of the Tennessee from joining forces with the Army of the Ohio under General Don Carlos Buell. Though Grant's men and the Confederates were fairly evenly matched, the Southerners with their flintlocks, shotguns, and pikes were far outgunned. The Union seemed poised to take the Mississippi River and capture the port of New Orleans, the Confederacy's biggest city.

On May 10, Federal troops commanded by McClellan attacked Norfolk and crucial Southern shipyards, overwhelming the Confederate defenders and forcing them to retreat toward Richmond. Barring a miraculous turn of events, northern Virginia would soon be overrun. But for some reason—maybe it was the relentless spring rains and the resulting miserable roads—McDowell, still in the field but now serving under McClellan, turned his men around and headed back toward Washington. For the moment, the Confederate capital was saved.

The clash that was shaping up in Virginia pitted 72,000 soldiers in Confederate gray against 150,000 invading bluecoats. General Joe Johnston seemed to have no solid battle plan to protect the city and no ideas for a counteroffensive. Unfortunately for Lee, Johnston was bedeviled by the same vanity and jealousy that had made Generals Floyd and Wise so hard to manage.

On May 23, Lee received rare good news in a dispatch from Stonewall Jackson. He'd won at Port Royal and captured a stock of medical supplies and ammunition. Only days later, however, the morning of May 27, McDowell started his march on Richmond. McClellan might move to connect with him and crush the capital. Soldiers and citizens there braced for the worst, but McDowell turned in the direction of Fredericksburg, again sparing the city. Lee chafed all the more at Johnston's inaction and sent an offer to assist him in the field, hoping it would prompt Johnston to act. When Johnston still seemed indecisive, Lee rode out to Johnston on May 31 to discuss how to protect Richmond from Federals coming up the Peninsula.

Shortly after Lee arrived, President Davis appeared on an impromptu inspection of his own. When Lee asked about the gunfire he heard in the distance, Johnston assured him it was only a skirmish between picket lines. Lee and the president rode toward the exchange to satisfy their curiosity, figuring it would be too dark soon to shoot anymore. But within moments they stumbled into the middle of a full-fledged battle.

McClellan's forces approached the Chickahominy River, where Johnston expected to hold them to the south bank because he didn't think their reinforcements could cross the river to meet them. When the support troops successfully made it across, the rebels began to give way. No one seemed to know what to do. To the left of Lee and Davis, the Federals were firing relentlessly. To their right, an even hotter contest blazed away. Wounded soldiers wandered aimlessly between the lines, and the Union men on the right seemed on the brink of breaking through. Lee restrained himself from acting, believing he was there only as an observer, but Davis took command, sending messengers with battlefield instructions to his generals.

Darkness put an end to the day's fighting, though not before one of Davis's bravest leaders, General Wade Hampton—a wealthy planter who bankrolled his own small army of infantry, cavalry, and artillery—was seriously wounded in the foot. General Johnston, shot in the chest and shoulder, was not expected to live, yet he survived and returned later to duty.

Johnston's retreat as McClellan came up the Peninsula left the Confederates dug in only five miles from Richmond. Union soldiers could see church steeples in the city. For some reason, the Federals chose to consolidate their gains and rest. That was as close as they would come to the Confederate capital.

Once all the casualties were tallied, Major General Gustavus Woodson Smith, a West Point graduate and Mexican War veteran, was left the ranking commander in the field. When he reported to Davis that night, the president asked Smith what he planned to do. General Smith acted as if he had no idea. He said the army might need to retreat further, though it was a scant five miles from that spot to the steps of the capitol. Or maybe they could hold their ground. Some historians believe Smith had what today would be called a nervous breakdown. He seemed to go back and forth between being frozen and being indecisive.

The impromptu war conference ended without firm plans. Davis and Lee returned to Richmond, their horses walking beside long lines of ambulances carrying the wounded back to the city. During the ride, Davis decided to relieve Smith and replace him with Lee immediately. He told the general to be ready to assume Smith's command, and as soon as Davis got home that night, he sent Smith the order.

When he took command of the army charged with protecting Richmond, Lee carried the further burden of having his invalid wife and two of their daughters caught behind enemy lines. As the fighting advanced through the countryside, Lee's family moved several times to safer quarters. Now they needed to move again, but they waited too long. On May 11, Mrs. Lee, Annie, and Mildred left White House for the neighboring plantation of Criss Cross. Before she drove off, Mary posted a note on the door:

*Northern soldiers who profess to reverence Washington, forbear to desecrate the home of his first married life, the property of his wife, now owned by her descendants.*

A GRANDDAUGHTER OF MRS. WASHINGTON

Within a week a Union patrol arrived at Criss Cross, which meant the wife of General Lee was behind enemy lines. The commanding officer, General Fitz-John Porter, had been a family friend and dinner guest at Arlington before the war. He assured Mary that she could pass safely through to the Confederates. With the general's permission she and her daughters moved to Marlbourne, the home of Edmund Ruffin, now also in Union hands, while the general arranged for her safe passage. Ruffin had fired the first shot at Fort Sumter.

Robert had told Mary repeatedly that it wasn't safe for her to join him in Richmond because he believed the capital would be invaded. Now she was technically a Union prisoner of war. Lee left the final decision to Mary about where she should live, and she wanted to be with Robert. On June 10, 1862, an unseasonably cold and wet day, Mary and her daughters arrived at the headquarters of General McClellan, who had taken over as general in chief at last from the venerable General Scott. McClellan gave Mary a pass that would get her through to her husband. General Lee sent an escort, Major Roy W. Mason, to meet his family at McClellan's headquarters with a carriage to take them to safety. Two Union officers on horseback, one holding a white flag of truce, led the women and Major Mason down the muddy road.

Around one o'clock in the afternoon, they met Confederate sentries, who sent for the watch officer. Meanwhile the sentry officer, Lieutenant Robert Haile of the Fifty-fifth Virginia Infantry, passed the time with the Union escorts and found them "men of refinement and sense." That night in his diary he wrote that one of the Federals offered his flask: "As I was wet and cold I thanked him and took a good pull at it. Found it to be nice whiskey."

A while later the watch commander, Captain Burke, came up and "after a good deal of talking and formalities Mrs. Lee was passed to our lines." Major Mason took her to a farmhouse nearby where Lee waited for her. They hadn't seen each other in more than a year; she'd never seen her husband in his general's uniform and never seen the beard he had grown while he was in western Virginia. The family went together to Richmond, where Mrs. Lee and the girls moved in with friends while General Lee returned to his headquarters at the Spotswood Hotel a few blocks away. They were home, after a fashion, and would rely on God's providence to see them through.

Though strategically unimportant, the battle at Antietam Creek near Sharpsburg, Maryland, Sept 17, 1862 was the first significant battle on Northern soil and the deadliest day in American history: 22,000 casualties and more than 3,500 dead, including these soldiers from a Louisiana regiment.

The battle of Gettysburg, Pennsylvania, July 1-3, 1863, marked the deepest penetration of Confederate forces into Northern territory, and a defeat from which the Army of Northern Virginia never recovered. These soldiers were among the 4,700 Union dead; more than 3,000 Confederates also died.

General Lee astride Traveller, his favorite horse. The American saddlebred gelding was purchased by the army quartermaster for Lee's use in western Virginia during the first months of the war. Lee later bought him from the government.

General Lee in his dress uniform with sash and sword, 1863.

## FOURTEEN

# Ancient Freedom

RICHMOND IN JUNE 1862 was far different from the city that General Lee had known all his life. During the first year of the war, its population quadrupled, sparking a shortage of living space, food, horses, furniture, clothing, glassware, building materials, and almost everything else. With trade slowed to a trickle by the naval blockade, and what little the South had being directed toward the war effort, carrying on normally would have been hard even if the population hadn't spiked. The city teemed with soldiers and the innkeepers, blacksmiths, outfitters, barflies, and others who followed in their wake. Prices for everything were breath-taking—when they were available at all. Still a tireless correspondent, Mrs. Lee started tearing sheets of paper in half and writing as small as her arthritic hands would allow. She asked

155

her correspondents to send "the *cheapest* writing paper of any kind" as well as knitting yarn for the general's socks, which was unavailable in Richmond at any price. Before the war was over, a spool of thread that had sold for pennies would cost four dollars and a drinking glass once worth a quarter or so, ten dollars.

Time and again Lee had been frustrated to see opportunities in the field squandered because Confederate military leaders failed to act. It seemed they were always waiting on more supplies, better weather, clearer intelligence, or something else they didn't have. At last Lee was in direct command, and he lost no time taking specific steps to reenergize, refocus, and engage his army.

Lee knew he couldn't keep the Federals out of Richmond indefinitely. The enemy had far more men than he could muster, plus unlimited reserves. Lee's alternative was to prepare a strong network of defensive earthworks around the capital so a small force could hold it, then go on the offensive against the Union in Maryland and Pennsylvania. This attack, Lee believed, would force the Federals to withdraw big blocks of troops from northern Virginia, relieving Richmond from the threat of invasion and capture. An offensive would also be a great morale booster for the Confederates, encouraging enlistment and reenlistment. Another goal was to shock the pro-war Northerners who had been personally unaffected by the war so far. There was a chance an invasion could turn public opinion in the North against continuing the fighting and toward leaving the Confederacy alone.

Lee had great confidence in well-dug and well-secured earthworks, and had insisted on them at Manassas. Soldiers despised digging. Some of them refused, insisting it wasn't work fit for a white man. Slaves and free blacks usually did the digging in the South. As he ordered excavations around Richmond, Granny Lee acquired another nickname as the "King of Spades." Yet for all their unpopularity, even the grumbling ranks would one day admit good earthworks were a godsend.

Soon Lee realized he would have to abandon his invasion plans for the time being because he couldn't gather enough troops to have any reasonable chance of success. Still determined to act, he planned an offensive to drive McClellan back down the Virginia Peninsula and give Richmond some relief. Taking command of the Confederate Army of the Potomac on June 1, Lee rechristened it the Army of Northern Virginia. Though only organized about a year, the army had by then absorbed several other units and was fortified by other brigades from across the Confederacy, giving Lee a total of about 56,000 officers and men.

The army saw its first action under Lee during a skirmish on June 25, 1862, at Oak Grove, when Union artillerymen trying to place their guns within range of Richmond were repelled by the rebels. That was the first of what would be six battles in seven days, pushing McClellan back down the Peninsula across the James River and far away from the capital. The first major battle of this Seven Days campaign, Lee's first battle command, occurred on June 26 near Mechanicsville, northeast of Richmond on the Chickahominy River. The Union army was camped on both sides of the river. Lee had left 25,000 men to guard Richmond, giving him roughly 30,000 in the field. McClellan stationed 65,000 troops around Richmond and had another 60,000 to meet Lee on the march.

Vastly outnumbered as he was, Lee knew a frontal assault

was hopeless. Instead he would attack the Union flank on the north side of the Chickahominy where there was only one corps, compared with four on the south bank. It was risky to concentrate his men on one side of the river when most of the enemy was on the other, but the general believed the element of surprise was worth the gamble. The lone Northern corps was commanded by General Fitz-John Porter, the family acquaintance who had seen Lee's wife and daughters to safety after they were caught in the Union advance. Against Porter, Lee sent the rising young star who was already one of his most trusted leaders, General Thomas "Stonewall" Jackson. He and his men arrived June 25 after the march from the Shenandoah Valley, but were late getting to their assigned positions. When fighting began the next day, they camped within earshot of the battle but stayed put, evidently in order to rest.

Hoping to salvage something of the day, Confederate General A. P. Hill attacked with disastrous results. Other commanders were waiting on Jackson, but Stonewall and his men never arrived. By nightfall Lee had been able to get only 14,000 of his 56,000 soldiers into the fight. It was another whole day before he finally connected with General Jackson. Lee didn't ask for an explanation about why Jackson was so late, and Jackson offered none.

Despite all the mistakes, the Confederate drive at Mechanicsville (also called the Battle of Beaver Dam Creek) achieved its bold objective of pushing McClellan and his huge army away from Richmond. McClellan assumed there were more Confederates than there actually were, and he made the strategic decision to fall back and protect his supply lines on the James River. This meant giving up the rail line that supported the troops around Richmond. McClellan then abandoned his emplacements on the Chickahominy and halted his assault on Richmond.

Jackson's delay cost Lee a clear victory, but McClellan was on the run and Lee lost no time in going after him. The next morning, Lee pursued the Federals down the Peninsula to a bog called Boatswain's Swamp. McClellan was headed for the James River. Once he got across, there would be no point in trying to chase him farther. The Federals could easily make a stand on the opposite bank and cut the rebels down as they tried to ford the river. Lee believed he could catch them before they reached the James by concentrating his divisions at Frayser's Farm near the town of Glendale. There he could cut off the enemy route to the river and divide the Union army in two.

In a scene too often repeated, Lee's carefully made plans depended on the element of surprise, careful coordination, and quick, precise movement. It was an engineer's way of solving a problem and a strategically sound one. The weakness was that the plans failed to account for the fact that most men, including other talented and respected generals, lacked Lee's level of order, discipline, and single-mindedness.

June 30 dawned cloudless and calm. The bluecoats were moving toward Malvern Hill, one of the estates of Lee's grandfather, Charles Carter. Federal gunboats on the river opened up, and Lee prepared to execute his maneuver to split McClellan's troops in half. At the crucial moment, however, the divisions commanded by Generals Benjamin Huger and Stonewall Jackson were nowhere to be seen. Afraid that the Union would retreat to the river landing where their position would be impregnable, Lee ordered an attack with the men he had. That meant 20,000 soldiers fought at Frayser's Farm while all the rest were somewhere off the line of battle waiting for instructions. Huger, it turned out, was delayed by huge trees felled across the road. Jackson had to fight his way through White Oak Swamp on his way across the Chickahominy.

Jackson ordered his men to make camp, apparently with no plans to ford the river and keep up the chase. General Wade Hampton reported that he had found a spot on the bank to build a bridge and that the Northern soldiers were resting just past the riverbank. Jackson agreed to build the bridge. Hampton had it done in short order, then crossed it and found the enemy still relaxing with no idea that the new temporary bridge was there. Jackson's strange response was to acknowledge Hampton's report, write a letter to his wife, and fall asleep without issuing any orders. As the sound of gunfire from Frayser's Farm grew louder, Jackson's staff tried to wake him but without success. When he finally sat down for supper, he fell asleep again with his mouth full of food.

Frayser's Farm, according to Freeman, "was one of the great lost opportunities in Confederate military history. It was the bitterest disappointment Lee had ever sustained, and one that he could not conceal. Victories in the field were to be registered, but two years of open campaign were not to produce another situation where envelopment seemed possible."

The seven-day chase forced McClellan to give up his attack on Richmond, but in spite of golden opportunities, Lee had not been able to strike a decisive blow. In the positive column, the

South captured 52 fieldpieces and more than 30,000 badly needed rifles, along with 10,000 soldiers taken prisoner. The cost, however, was 20,000 Confederate casualties, half of them killed, mortally wounded, or permanently disabled. As Lee reported, "Under ordinary circumstances the Federal army should have been destroyed." Some politicians and commentators found fault with Lee's generalship, but the public hailed him as the hero who saved Richmond. Granny Lee and the King of Spades were forgotten.

For the rest of July and most of August, Lee had a six-week break from rigorous battle. He let the army rest and regain its health with light duty and generous rations. There was still the matter of how to replenish his forces. A dribble of new conscripts and healing wounded came in, but the Confederacy remained chronically undermanned. Meanwhile, the Union army in the valley reorganized into a new Army of Virginia under General John Pope. Stung by McClellan's defeat, the Federals called up another 300,000 new recruits.

Lee set three objectives for the next phase of the war. First, make the defenses around Richmond as strong as possible in order to hold it safely with the fewest men. Second, protect the Virginia Central Railroad right-of-way to the fertile Shenandoah Valley that was his supply lifeline for provisions. Third, figure out how he could spare Stonewall Jackson's division to go after Pope in the valley and still defend against another attack on the Peninsula by McClellan.

Lee drew up plans to attack Pope at a point where the Rappahannock and Rapidan river valleys came together like a V pointing east, catching the Federals between the two rivers and besting an army of 65,000 or more with a force 20,000 smaller. He set August 18 for the assault, yet when the morning came, some units were not in place. One day passed, then two. The Confederates still weren't ready. By then the Federals knew what their opponents were about and moved to meet every thrust. Papers captured from General Pope's field headquarters revealed that McClellan was on the way to join him; their combined forces would hopelessly overwhelm Lee's men. Lee responded with a plan to push Pope away from McClellan and cut his supply line, the Orange and Alexandria Railroad.

In spite of General Jackson's poor and still unexplained performance during the Seven Days, Lee put him in charge of marching west up the Rappahannock Valley, the northern part of the V, to get behind Pope and cut off his railroad access to Washington. When it looked as if Pope's men were about to move, Lee ordered General James Longstreet to reinforce Jackson. On August 27, Lee received word that Jackson had reached the railroad, captured two trains, torn up a section of track, and was headed for the Federal storehouses at Manassas, site of the Confederate victory the year before. This success put Lee just where he wanted to be, behind Pope's forces and between them and Washington. The next day Pope counterattacked. Lee had hoped Longstreet would arrive in time to help Jackson absorb the blow, but Longstreet's forces took two days to travel the twenty-eight miles to the battlefront.

Finally Longstreet marched into position on August 29, but failed to execute Lee's order to attack, insisting he needed more reconnaissance first. True to form, Lee hesitated to insist on advancing when the field officer who would lead thought it was a bad idea. Three times Lee ordered an attack, three times Longstreet resisted, and three times Lee deferred. Longstreet finally launched his offensive the next day. Together he and Jackson pushed hard against the bluecoats. As darkness came and rain started to fall, the Federals retreated to the safety of their Washington defenses. Within two weeks General Pope was stripped of his command and posted to Minnesota, where he spent the rest of the war trying to justify his defeat.

Lee lost no time trying to capitalize on his victory at Manassas. He returned again to the idea of marching on Maryland and Pennsylvania, confident that the Union would not attack Richmond if Confederate troops were on U.S. soil. There was also a chance that Maryland might be persuaded to abandon the North for the South, giving Lee new sources of troops and provisions. If Maryland changed sides, the Union capital would be completely surrounded by Confederate territory. Lee carried on despite having both hands in splints; they were badly sprained in a fall. He'd been standing beside Traveller, a big grey American saddlebred gelding that his quartermaster had found for him during the western Virginia campaign, and tried to grab the reins when the horse was spooked. Two days before that, a Federal sharpshooter had grazed his cheek.

Looking ahead at an offensive against the North, Lee had to consider again whether he could spare men from the defense of Richmond and whether he could equip and supply them in enemy territory. He decided to move aggressively, attacking east of the Blue Ridge Mountains, which was more exposed and dangerous than the western approach but closer to Washington and, he hoped, more threatening.

Confederate troops waded and swam across the Potomac onto hostile ground beginning September 5, 1862. By the seventh, the army occupied the town of Frederick, Maryland, and Lee had set up his headquarters nearby. Determined to appeal to Marylanders any way he could, Lee issued strict orders against harassing the citizens and posted guards at the shops. On September 8, the general issued a proclamation to the people of the state:

> No constraint upon your free will is intended; no intimidation will be allowed within the limits of this army, at least. Marylanders shall once more enjoy their ancient freedom of thought and speech. We know no enemies among you, and will protect all, of every opinion. It is for you to decide your destiny freely and without constraint. This army will respect your choice, whatever it may be; and while the Southern people will rejoice to welcome you to your natural position among them, they will only welcome you when you come of your own free will.

True to his long-standing beliefs, Lee made no effort to defend slavery, only to remind the citizens of their state's rights to decide matters for themselves. Marylanders were at least somewhat divided. Some townspeople brought food to the Confederate soldiers, while others walked by holding their noses.

On September 15, Lee established a defensive position north and east of the town of Sharpsburg, Maryland, with

Antietam Creek to the front. Before daylight on the seventeenth, Union batteries opened up on them. This time Lee didn't offer subordinates the chance to make decisions that risked delays or lost opportunities. Though still unable to ride because of his bandaged hands, Lee took complete command of the battlefield, artfully moving his troops back and forth along an inner line of defense to hold back every Union advance. Outnumbering him two to one, McClellan nevertheless failed to break the Confederate line. When he saw he couldn't advance any farther, Lee organized an orderly withdrawal back across the Potomac and home to Virginia. Strategists hailed Lee's work for defending a line even though he was so outnumbered, but his retreat put an end to the Confederate offensive.

Lincoln was furious at McClellan for failing to overrun the rebels and even madder that he didn't chase them across the Potomac. On November 7, he relieved McClellan of his command.

Strategically, the Battle of Sharpsburg at Antietam Creek was relatively unimportant. Historically, it was and remains the deadliest day in the history of American warfare. Of the 75,000 Federals and 38,000 Confederates engaged, there were more than 12,000 Northern losses, including more than 2,000 killed, and 10,000 Southern losses, including more than 1,500 dead. According to one eyewitness, bodies were laid out in rows like birds at the end of a day's hunting.

Lee gave his men another badly needed rest and turned again to matters of manpower and recruitment, reorganizing his command into two corps, one under Longstreet and the other under Jackson. On September 23, President Lincoln announced the

Emancipation Proclamation to take effect the following New Year's Day, despite his campaign position not to interfere with slavery in states where it was already established. Some critics believed Lincoln timed his announcement to take political advantage of the bloody battle at Sharpsburg. Others saw it as confirmation that the president was out to dismantle the Constitution and eviscerate the laws and traditions of states' rights.

Lee expected the enemy to attack again, but hoped to hold them off until winter weather set in. McClellan was replaced on November 9 by Major General Ambrose E. Burnside. The new Union commander would not lapse into the indecision and ineffectiveness that had brought down his predecessor. On November 17, only days after Burnside assumed his post, scouts reported Federals moving against Fredericksburg from across the Rappahannock River. To fend them off, Lee positioned artillery behind the town on Marye's Heights, crowned by a fine brick mansion.

On December 11, Federals installed pontoon bridges in three places along the snow-covered banks of the Rappahannock, preparing to attack with 125,000 men against about 78,000 defenders. In spite of his superior numbers, Burnside failed in his assault. He launched a frontal attack against the artillery on Marye's Heights so that Lee's cannons could pound him between the edge of town and the base of the Heights. Also between the blue invaders and their objective was Telegraph Road, with a sunken roadbed that exposed them like ducks in a shooting gallery. A ditch near the road provided some cover, but it was ineffective against the well-aimed Confederate shells. After sustaining heavy losses, the Union army retreated. Watching the bluecoats go, Lee turned to Longstreet and observed, "It is well that war is so terrible—we should grow too fond of it."

At one point when Southern cannoneers were changing out artillery pieces, the Federals took the movement of their wagons for a retreat. When the Federals surged ahead, the new guns mowed them down. By the morning of December 14, the fighting had slowed to a few rifle pops here and there, but the next day the invaders built earthworks and rifle pits as if they were going to attack again. To Lee's surprise and relief, the sun came up December 15 on an empty field: the enemy had withdrawn. The Federals logged 12,000 casualties against about 5,000 for the Confederacy. Southern soldiers scrounged uniforms, shoes, and blankets left behind, and captured 11,000 small arms. Lee was uncharacteristically buoyant after the victory. The Charleston *Mercury* reported that the general was "jubilant, almost off-balance, and seemingly desirous of embracing everyone who calls on him."

The South had held its own against all odds, but the year brought heavy personal tragedy to General Lee. During the Seven Days, McClellan had briefly used the White House as his field headquarters. Before the end of the year, in spite of Mrs. Lee's stern note on the door, the house was burned to the ground; only its blackened chimneys remained. Rooney's two-year-old son, Lee's only grandchild, died of tuberculosis that winter. Rooney's second child, born prematurely, died only weeks later. Lee's precious daughter Annie, his Little Raspberry, had died at twenty-three of typhoid fever while on a visit to the mineral baths in Warrenton Springs.

Words were scant comfort to his sorrowful wife, but they

were all he had to offer, along with a reminder that everything was in God's hands and that He knew best even when life was so heart wrenching: "I cannot express the anguish I feel at the death of our sweet Annie. . . . But God, in this as in all things, has mingled mercy with the blow, in selecting that one best prepared to leave us. May you be able to join me in saying, 'His will be done!'"

In times past it was Mary who'd encouraged Robert in his faith. Now he had the confidence and assurance to encourage her: "I wish I could give you any comfort, but beyond our hope in the great mercy of God, and the belief that He takes her at the time and place where it is best for her to go, there is none. When I reflect on all she will escape in life, brief and painful at the best, and all we may hope she will enjoy with her sainted grandmother, I cannot wish her back."

He revisited his affirmation that God was in control in a letter to Mary, sent from the field of victory at Fredericksburg on Christmas Day:

What a cruel thing war is to separate and destroy families and friends, and mar the purest joys and happiness God has granted us in this world; to fill our hearts with hatred instead of love for our neighbors, and to devastate the face of this beautiful world! I pray that on this day when only peace and goodwill are preached to mankind, better thoughts may fill the hearts of our enemies and turn them to peace.

Four days later, on December 29, Lee filed a deed of manumission at the Spotsylvania County, Virginia, courthouse freeing all the Arlington slaves in accordance with the terms of Mr. Custis's will. "They are entitled to their freedom," he said, "and I wish to give it to them."

The last day of 1862, Lee issued a message to his men. It had been a brutal year, but one ending with a great and unqualified victory. Better than most, Lee knew how hard the year ahead would be. His soldiers would be poorly dressed, poorly provisioned, and weary from fighting. But for now he could look away from the bad news, pause, and give thanks for the blessings that were theirs:

> The general commanding takes this occasion to express to the officers and soldiers of the arm his highest appreciation of the fortitude, valor, and devotion, displayed by them, which under the blessing of Almighty God have added the victory of Fredericksburg to their long list of triumphs. . . . [This victory] only augments the admiration with which the commanding general regards the prowess of his troops, and increases his gratitude to Him who hath given us the victory. . . . The signal manifestations of Divine Mercy that have distinguished the eventful and glorious campaign . . . give assurance of hope that under the guidance of the same Almighty hand the coming year will be no less fruitful.

# FIFTEEN

# The Smell of Victory

SHORTLY AFTER HIS defeat at Fredericksburg, General Burnside launched another offensive that became infamous as the Mud March. Trying to advance, Federal troops sank in roads that snow, sleet, and driving rain had turned into a hopeless quagmire. Northern politicians and news editors harshly criticized his ability, which made Burnside furious. He pressed Lincoln either to court-martial the disobedient officers under his command or to accept his resignation. It wasn't a hard choice for the president. He relieved Burnside on January 26, 1863, sent him off to Ohio, and replaced him with one of Burnside's chief critics, Major General Joseph Hooker.

While Hooker settled into place, the weather remained fierce. Lee let his weary men rest, firmed up his supply lines, and continued the unending effort to fill out his ranks. "Our salvation will depend on the next four months," he told Davis, "and yet I cannot get even regular promotions made to fill vacancies in regiments, while Congress seems to be laboring to pass laws to get easy places for some favorites or constituents, or get others out of active service." One problem was that there were too many loopholes for conscripts with friends in high places or with the money to hire a replacement.

Confederate legislators improved matters somewhat by raising the maximum draft age from thirty-five to forty-five. Solving one problem created another one, however, as even more men had to have food, shelter, uniforms, arms, and ammunition. Out of one batch of 1,500 Louisiana recruits, 400 stood barefoot in the January snow. Lee was shocked to learn that privateers were offering shoes at outrageous prices. He asked Davis if they could legally force merchants to sell at a fair figure, though some soldiers wouldn't be able to wear shoes for days or weeks until their bruised and swollen feet could heal.

General Hooker stirred and demonstrated here and there, but soon Lee could see that his new adversary would stay put for the most part until spring. After six weeks, Lee was finally able to take the bandages off his hands, though the right one was still painful and swollen. He managed to dress, eat, and ride with the left hand alone. The weather continued miserable through February, with snow knee deep and temperatures relentlessly cold. The men had just enough to eat, except when the supply train was delayed by ice and snow and their meager ration was cut even more. General Lee could easily have spent the winter nearby in Richmond, sitting with his wife and daughters by the fireside, but that wasn't his way. He insisted on camping with his men, though his servant Perry, once a dining steward at Arlington, built a fireplace and chimney at one end of his tent.

By that time, elegant dinners at Arlington were a distant memory, the house and grounds sinking steadily into ruin at the hands of Federal occupiers. Edwin M. Stanton, Lincoln's secretary of war, had gone out of his way to make the place as hard and expensive to restore as possible, assuming Lee ever got the chance. The Union government built a huge stable complex for military horses and mules on the property, along with a large convalescent hospital. On Mr. Custis's picnic grounds at Arlington Spring, a massive settlement for free and homeless slaves called Freedman's Village eventually housed two thousand residents.

For the first time since his malaria attack of 1849, General Lee fell seriously ill in late March 1863. Chest pains and sharp, shooting pains in his arm and back sent him to bed weak and miserable. Based on his symptoms, he could have had pericarditis, angina, or, most likely, a heart attack. Bedridden for days, Lee was making his way around camp again by about April 1, but it was another two weeks before he resumed his daily routine. Pain, weakness, and a sense of exhaustion stayed with him to some degree for the rest of the war.

On April 9, Lee once again recommended an offensive in Maryland as soon as roads would allow. He set May 1 to begin the campaign unless Hooker moved before then. Two days ahead of his schedule, Federal forces crossed the Rappahannock on pontoon boats in the fog. There were about 62,500 Southern troops to stand against 138,000 invaders moving toward Chancellorsville, where they could flank the Confederate position. Lee ordered his commander there, General R. H. Anderson, to dig in securely and cook two days' rations.

Despite the hard lesson of Sharpsburg, Lee took the risk of dividing his forces into three. He reinforced his old position on Marye's Heights above Fredericksburg, extending his line southeast to keep Hooker from getting between him and Richmond. Lee held the new extension three miles long with only 14,000 men. As General Lee considered a counterstrike from the west at Chancellorsville, Jackson suggested a full-blown surprise assault from the same spot.

Lee took Jackson's advice. Early on the morning of May 2, Jackson and his men moved out, marching all day and into the night. Near Wilderness Church, he found Federals in camp cooking their supper and routed them completely. General Lee's elation at the news was tempered by a follow-up report that Jackson had been shot by his own men, once in the right hand and twice in the left arm. Though the injuries didn't seem serious, Lee declared, "Any victory is dearly bought which deprives us of the services of General Jackson, even for a short time." He dashed off a note of encouragement to his friend: "Could I have directed events, I should have chosen, for the good of the country, to have been disabled in your stead. I congratulate you upon the victory which is due to your skill and energy."

The Confederates gradually gained the upper hand around Chancellorsville despite too frequent instances of confusion and miscommunication. When Union brigades began to retreat, Lee planned a night advance to stop them before they could recross the Rappahannock. To his disappointment, the invaders slipped away before he could catch them. Next he turned his army toward the town and Hooker's main force, but by the morning of May 6, the Federals had slipped away once more.

At great risk Lee had divided his command into three, then scored so convincingly that it was a full year before the Union tried to invade Virginia again. Douglas Southall Freeman considered Chancellorsville "nearly a flawless battle . . . undoubtedly the most remarkable victory [Lee] ever achieved, and it increased greatly his well-established reputation both in the eyes of the enemy and of the South."

Lee gave all the glory to God. In his general order issued after the battle he reminded his men,

> While this glorious victory entitles you to the praise and gratitude of the nation, we are especially called upon to return our grateful thanks to the only Giver of victory for the signal deliverance He had wrought.
>
> It is therefore earnestly recommended that the troops unite, on Sunday next, in ascribing unto the Lord of hosts the glory due unto his name.

The inspired victory at Chancellorsville came at a grave personal cost for General Lee. Stonewall Jackson's wounds developed a massive infection. The field surgeons' only remedy was amputation, after which the doctors reported that he was improving. Just as he seemed out of danger, Jackson caught pneumonia and faded rapidly. Lee prayed earnestly on his knees that Jackson might live. But on May 10, the Sunday that Lee had encouraged his troops to give thanks to God for their victory, word came that General Thomas J. Jackson was dead at thirty-nine.

Saddened as he was, Lee lost no time replacing Jackson and planning his next move. He reorganized his army into three corps: one under Longstreet as before, one under Jackson's second in command, R. S. Ewell, and a third new corps under A. P. Hill. Then he returned to his strategy for invading Maryland and Pennsylvania.

Lee thought the benefits of a successful invasion made it worth another try. For one, the investment in food and fodder could bring handsome returns by giving his forces a new source for supplies. The Virginia countryside where the army had camped and fought for months was stripped clean. He also believed an offensive would divert Northern attention and resources away from other theaters of the war where things were going badly for the South. Nashville had fallen, making it the first Southern state capital in enemy hands, and the rebels kept losing ground in Tennessee. Even more serious, Union forces commanded by General U. S. Grant had Vicksburg under siege. A loss there would give Federals control of the whole Mississippi River. Furthermore, Lee still figured that a convincing thrust northward would encourage Northern politicians to consider a truce.

Capturing the Pennsylvania state capital at Harrisburg would meet all of Lee's objectives. In early June he started shifting his army from the Rappahannock to the Shenandoah Valley and into Maryland. Though it was enemy territory, Maryland bordered both Virginia and the District of Columbia, and it was a slave-holding state. Surely sons of the South would find allies there.

The march was hot and miserable. Columns of soldiers sent up clouds of white dust that settled on their faces, rifles, uniforms, horses, wagons, everything. The only places not caked in white were the rivulets of sweat running down their skin. Troops and animals were constantly thirsty. Crossing the Potomac offered a rare moment of relief as the weary brigades stripped naked and waded by the thousands through waist-deep water "yelling & screaming like school children," balancing their clothing and supplies on their heads.

Virginia native John E. Dooley had left his studies at Georgetown College to enlist in the infantry. He later recalled the "terrible [trek] along the scorched and blazing plains of Virginia" and the toll it took on his fellow soldiers:

> Angry was the glare of the sun during those fearful days in June, as it flashed upon our ranks and fiercely smote again and again the burning temples of our fagged and fainting soldiers. Choking, blinding were the clouds of dust that rose from beneath the army's unsteady tread; parching was that unquenchable thirst which dried the tongue to its very roots. The men fell by tens and twenties, nay by hundreds along the dusty roadsides.

By the time the whole column had crossed into hostile territory on June 25, 1863, the soldiers had already fought several engagements. The first was with General Stuart's cavalry at

Brandy Station on June 9 near Culpeper, Virginia. It was reportedly the biggest cavalry engagement ever, with 9,500 horsemen under Stuart against 8,000 cavalry and 3,000 infantry led by Major General Alfred Pleasonton. One Confederate casualty was Major General Fitzhugh Lee, Robert's son Rooney, shot in the thigh by a new kind of bullet with a zinc cap designed to come off and fester in the wound. Fortunately he was hit at such close range that the bullet went completely through.

To advance as fast as possible, Lee separated his corps. Ewell, stationed farthest west, went north toward Hagerstown, Maryland, in the direction of Harrisburg. Longstreet led his column north up the east side of the Blue Ridge Mountains, keeping his cavalry between the enemy and Hill's forces marching up the Shenandoah Valley west of the mountains. Once Hill was through the valley, Longstreet was to cut west through a mountain pass and follow as a rear guard. After several small skirmishes, the Confederates arrived in Pennsylvania on June 26.

Southern soldiers were impressed with the neat, prosperous-looking farms and abundant crops of Pennsylvania. Some of them had always assumed that successful agriculture depended on slave labor, yet here were fine, solid houses, miles of well-maintained fencerows, and people who seemed to have everything they could want. The people themselves, however, were another story. As one Confederate private wrote to his sister, Pennsylvania had "some of the finest land in it in the world and some of the ugliest women I ever saw." Despite strict orders not to steal from the locals as the Federals had done in the South, Confederate soldiers ransacked stores along the way, commandeered animals and equipment, and "took everything they could lay their hands on in the eating line."

Lee set up his headquarters on a picnic ground outside Chambersburg, with some advance columns heading north toward Carlisle and York. Jeb Stuart's cavalry was assigned to screen the northbound infantry, keeping to the east between them and the Federals to protect the Confederate right flank. Stuart had more ambitious plans for himself. Fresh from his victory at Brandy Station and brimming with confidence, he wanted to maneuver behind Hooker and harass him. Lee approved the change, but only under the condition that as soon as Hooker crossed the Potomac into Maryland, Stuart would hurry back to protect Ewell's infantry.

By June 27 the Confederate army was at Carlisle on the road to Harrisburg. Day after day the temperatures hit a hundred degrees in the shade, while nights in the open were surprisingly chilly. Rain added to the misery, since the Southerners had few tents or blankets and couldn't build campfires that might be spotted by Northern pickets. Lee told Ewell to take Harrisburg if his force was large enough. General Lee needed the protection of Stuart's cavalry to continue northward, but since he'd gone off to pester Hooker, Stuart hadn't reported in. Lee never expected him to be absent so long, but he assumed Hooker was still in Virginia, since he had specifically ordered Stuart to rush back if Hooker threatened.

The fact was that Hooker was no longer anywhere in the field. The morning of June 28, Lincoln relieved him of command and replaced him with Major General George Gordon Meade. Lee got word of the change two days after learning that his son Rooney had been captured and was a prisoner of war. Rooney had been at his father-in-law's estate, Hickory Hill, recovering from his wound. On June 26 a Union raiding party burst into the plantation office where Rooney lay, picked him up on his mattress, and hauled him off in the commandeered family carriage.

Lee paced back and forth, uncharacteristically ill at ease, waiting on Stuart in order to continue his advance. The cavalry had not been able to turn the Union flank because as the Confederates moved north, the Federals moved with them, never giving Stuart room to wedge in between them. Seeing a chance to capture a big Union supply train, Stuart and his men rode off to do that, abandoning their flanking move and giving Lee no word about enemy troop movement.

It was June 29 when Lee received the shocking news from a spy that Union troops under Meade were already across the Potomac and headed straight for them. He couldn't wait any longer for his absent cavalry, though he felt exposed and blind without it. General Meade, an old acquaintance of Lee, seldom made mistakes, and he capitalized quickly when his opponent slipped. Caught unaware by Stuart's failure to report, Lee was furious. It was, his aides said, one of the few times in his life when his legendary self-control deserted him.

Lee acted fast to consolidate his forces near Cashtown. As the brigades assembled there, a North Carolina brigade under Brigadier General J. J. Pettigrew advanced toward a community eight miles to the east, a county seat of 2,400 called Gettysburg. Pettigrew heard that a supply of shoes was there, and he wanted it for his men. Gettysburg was a hardworking, orderly town of sturdy brick buildings and airy frame houses. Several highways crossed there, and it was a stop on the railroad to Hanover. In years past, Gettysburg had also been a link in the Underground Railroad, helping runaway slaves escape to free states.

General Henry Heth's division, under A. P. Hill, approached the city's outskirts on June 30 but withdrew when they saw Union cavalry ahead of them. That was another surprise. Lee, again counting on Stuart to keep him abreast of Union positions, was thunderstruck at the news. The next day, in spite of Lee's specific order not to attack until the whole army was assembled, A. P. Hill opened fire, supposedly to test the Union position. When other commanders heard gunfire, they committed troops as well, though Lee held off ordering a general attack because he had no cavalry and because Longstreet's corps had been delayed.

Around noon, Lee arrived, annoyed at first that Hill had started his offensive prematurely. He asked every officer he met, "Have you heard anything from General Stuart? Any news about the cavalry?" But once he saw momentum building in his favor, he decided he could win on the battlefield even without Longstreet's troops or Stuart's cavalry. Lee called for the advance to continue.

Through the blazing afternoon heat, waves of Confederates attacked while "yelling like demons." One-on-one combat was fierce and bloody for both sides, with casualties up to 70 percent in some units. Heth lost 2,300 men in thirty minutes. The colors of the Twenty-sixth North Carolina Infantry were carried by fourteen standard bearers as one was hit and another grabbed it from his falling hands. A Mississippi private described the slaughter around him: "I could have walked a half or three quarters of a mile on the dead soldiers of the enemy and not have put my feet on the ground. In some places they were lying three deep." After early hesitations and setbacks, the Confederates rolled forward, flattening fields of golden wheat before crossing Willoughby Run northwest of town. The defenders tried to make a stand in the buildings of the Lutheran seminary on a ridge along the western outskirts, but their forces crumbled and fell back, retreating through the streets and out the other side of town.

Musket and artillery fire mowed down ragged chunks of ripe wheat, flax, oats and corn. Men advanced and retreated through hellish scenes, stumbling over headless torsos, bloody limbs, bodies by the thousands, and worst of all, horribly wounded soldiers dying in agony. One soldier brought a canteen to another who, his jaw torn off, tried to drink through a wound in his throat. Another had his arm severed at the shoulder socket; another had his leg bone sticking out his thigh; another had the top of his head missing and brains cascading down his face. The heat made their suffering all the more desperate. Deadly infection killed when wounds themselves did not.

Directly south of Gettysburg was Cemetery Hill, with Culp's Hill just to the east. Running south from Cemetery Hill was Cemetery Ridge. The three formations together were shaped like a fishhook, with Culp's Hill as the barb and the southern end of the ridge as the eyelet. From his observation point to the northwest, Lee could see Federals scrambling up Cemetery Hill in disarray, confused, disorganized, and in no shape to defend their position.

For the first time Union soldiers had to hold onto their own soil, and at last the Confederates were the invaders. Over the course of the next few days, however, this situation worked against

Lee and his men in two ways. First, it inspired the Federals to fight harder. Second, it lured the Confederates into a false sense of security and dulled their resolve.

Even so, Lee's army collected five thousand prisoners in its sweep through town, and the smell of victory was in the air. If only the Confederates could roll on up the hill before the bluecoats got situated, they would control the high ground, almost certainly win the battle, and occupy Gettysburg. Culp's Hill and the ridge stood empty, inviting Lee's men forward. Then it would be on to Harrisburg—unless Lincoln wanted to talk peace now! Alexander Stephens, vice president of the Confederate States, waited at a checkpoint for permission to call on Lincoln if Lee established himself in Pennsylvania.

Lee sent orders for General Ewell to take the hill immediately, then waited anxiously for the sound of Confederate gunfire. Critical hours passed. Lee watched with alarm as the Union troops organized themselves and called up reinforcements. Finally around six o'clock in the afternoon, Lee rode to Ewell's headquarters. On the way, he passed Ewell's men building campfires and cooking their supper.

As he would have done in orders to Stonewall Jackson, Lee had directed Ewell to take the hill "if practicable," leaving the final decision to the commander in charge of executing the order. This again was Lee's way of leading, a combination of courtesy, humility, and an assumption that everybody else was as dedicated, sharp, and tireless as he was. But Ewell was used to executing specific commands as ordered. General Lee had ordered an immediate attack "if practicable," and Ewell didn't deem it practicable. His men were tired, and it would soon be dark. Freeman takes the inaction another step, asserting that Lee found Ewell "paralyzed by irresolution" and that he had "lost the will to act." Whatever the reason, a phenomenal opportunity was lost, and the Army of Northern Virginia would never have another like it.

That night, wounded men from both sides filled every barn, church, and building of any size. Women of the town bravely volunteered to help overworked doctors give what comfort they could to Union and Confederate alike. Mary McAllister, whose family owned a general store in town, went to a church down the street to nurse Federal casualties. A doctor sent her to find some wine, which she hid under her apron so soldiers on the street wouldn't see it. She returned just in time to give a badly wounded officer one sip before he died. Like many other women, Mary kept mementos—diaries, photos, letters, and pocketbooks—for the soldiers, who knew they'd soon be captured if they lived long enough and didn't want the precious tokens lost. Some volunteers wrote letters for the patients to their families back home telling of their capture and, too often, of their own approaching deaths.

"They carried the wounded in there as fast as they could," Miss McAllister wrote of that long, gruesome night. Soon the church was filled to overflowing, with some of the casualties on pew cushions on the floor. "I went to doing what they told me to do, wetting cloths and putting them on the wounds and helping. Every pew was full; some sitting, some lying, some leaning on others. They cut off legs and arms and threw them out of the windows. Every morning the dead were laid on the platform in a sheet or blanket and carried away."

In light of the lost opportunity on July 1, Lee's new plan was to attack from Seminary Ridge, depending heavily on Longstreet's fresh troops that had come up too late to fight the first day. Longstreet didn't like the idea, arguing that he should circle around the hill instead and try to get between the Union brigades and Washington. Lee listened but said nothing. The next morning Longstreet pressed his point again, and again Lee remained silent. Seeing Longstreet's men moving into position, Lee rode through the dank, heavy dawn air to Ewell to coordinate the advance.

Lee waited through the early morning with no action from Longstreet. At ten o'clock, Lee rode back to check on the situation and saw the men out of formation, resting on the grass. When he finally found Longstreet, Lee ordered an attack immediately, but Longstreet said he was waiting on reinforcements due within the hour. More time dragged by before Longstreet moved out—so much time that battlefield conditions had changed since Lee issued his orders. Lee had expected Longstreet to be on the march at 8:30 that morning and it was now 4:00 p.m. Following Lee's exact directive in light of current troop dispositions would be suicidal, but Longstreet, like a pouty child, insisted that if Lee was going to criticize his command, he'd do precisely what he was ordered to do. Lee had also been misled by faulty reconnaissance, and he expected his commanders to adjust for such problems on the spot. Thus another day ended with a historic opportunity lost, and in those twenty-four hours the Union army strengthened its position exponentially.

Even though the Confederates didn't press on as Lee wanted them to do, the second day at Gettysburg was the bloodiest of the battle, which itself would be the bloodiest of the war. Wounded soldiers were scattered everywhere in the field, screaming through the night in pain and begging pitifully for water. Those who made it to the tent hospitals fared only a little better. At least they could get water and something to eat, and maybe a little wine or whiskey. With so many casualties and limited supplies, the doctors couldn't do much to treat a wound in the relentless heat except to amputate in hopes of avoiding a fatal infection. The bone saws hacked away day and night, with military bands playing in shifts for hours on end to cover the screams.

For all the casualties he'd taken, Lee had inflicted about as many on his enemies, and he still held out hope that he could win Gettysburg. He had traveled so far, been so near to triumph twice in two days, and he saw great military and political advantages from a successful assault. Circumstances had robbed him of an easy victory; now he would get it the hard way.

The night of July 2, Stuart and the cavalry returned at last. Lee sent Longstreet orders to resume his attack the next morning after a massive artillery bombardment designed to pave the way. In a bad bit of timing, a raging case of diarrhea attacked Lee that night. Nevertheless he was up at dawn, waiting for Longstreet to move. Everything else would key off his march.

Once more, Lee waited in vain. He rode to his stubborn general's headquarters and had scarcely dismounted when Longstreet started arguing again for a flanking move. When Lee repeated his order, Longstreet countered with the suggestion that his division under General George Pickett, as the freshest body of troops, should lead a charge up the center of the line with full artillery support.

Why Lee put up with Longstreet's blatant insubordination in the middle of a battle is difficult to imagine. Maybe a combination of illness, his long-set habit of deferring to field commanders, and all the other issues and decisions crowding his mind prompted him to let the matter go. Whatever the reason, Lee's immediate need was to contact Ewell to say the advance was delayed. Just then Ewell opened fire, and it was too late. Finding no support, Ewell tapered off. Then his men, along with the full complement of artillery, waited hours in the baking sun for Longstreet to do something. One soldier no doubt spoke for many when he swore it was the hottest weather he'd felt in his life.

After noon, the gunners finally got word from Longstreet to open fire, but even then the message implied he wouldn't advance if the artillery barrage didn't make success likely. The cannons roared to a deafening crescendo, but Longstreet held back. Artillerymen fired until they bled freely from both ears, their gun wagons in splinters from relentless blasting and recoil. They reported their ammunition running low, fearful they wouldn't have enough left to support the advance if it ever came. General Pickett begged Longstreet for permission to attack. Without a word Longstreet nodded his head, and Pickett's men surged forward. When Longstreet heard that the artillery was short of powder, he tried to call Pickett back, but the charge went on.

Pickett's brigade charged up Cemetery Ridge into withering fire, supposedly the vanguard of a massive Confederate assault. But at the critical moment, no other brigades were ordered in support. Sending one message after another to Longstreet, calling frantically for help, Pickett made it with a few others to the abandoned first line of Federal guns. Without reinforcements he had no choice but to retreat down the hill to the safety of Seminary Ridge, leaving two-thirds of his men on the field killed or captured. Anguished and distraught, Pickett saw Lee on his horse and rushed over to report his failure to take Cemetery Ridge.

"Come, General Pickett," Lee assured him, "this has been my fight and upon my shoulders rests the blame. The men and officers of your command have written the name of Virginia today as high as it has ever been written before."

Physically and emotionally spent, Lee returned to his headquarters late that night. It had been perhaps the most devastating day of his life. His careful plans had been flagrantly disregarded, his orders ignored, resulting in thousands of men hurt or killed with little to show for it. His voice was so choked with feeling, he could hardly speak. Even the iron self-control of R. E. Lee could not hold back such a flood of emotion. Yet he never pointed a finger, never blamed anyone but himself.

"Yes, it has been a sad, sad day for us," he said. "I never saw troops behave more magnificently than Pickett's division of Virginians did in that grand charge upon the enemy. And if they had been supported as they were to have been—but, for some reason not yet explained to me, were not—we would have held the position and the day would have been ours. Too bad. *Too bad.* Oh TOO BAD!"

Witnesses could scarcely describe the aftermath of the battle. Entire stands of trees shattered by rifle and artillery fire continued to die for more than a year. Withdrawing armies left thousands of dead to be buried, their bodies already black and swollen to twice their size in the remorseless sun. Shirt buttons popped as fabric stretched like sausage casing and finally gave way. Facial features were unrecognizable so that some of the dead were unknown. Hurrying to get bodies in the ground, burial details dug shallow trenches and arranged corpses in long rows without coffins or even blankets. Many of the Union dead were shoeless; the rebels had scavenged the Gettysburg shoes they'd never had the chance to buy. Dead men and horses littered the streets, which were cleared as soon as possible and spread with quicklime to offset the stench. In and around town for days, the smell was so overpowering that passersby would suddenly fall to their knees and vomit.

Lee retreated, recrossing the Potomac and, on August 4, the Rappahannock, putting him back where he started. The campaign cost the Confederacy more than 23,000 casualties, including 4,700 dead. Union losses overall were about the same with 3,100 killed. In a letter to his uncle written July 24, General Longstreet admitted that his insubordination and failure had cost them Gettysburg, that "all the responsibility" was his. Later he traded that position for an aggressive strain of historical revisionism, but Lee never made a public statement challenging or condemning him.

General Lee wrote a note to his wife on the way home, announcing his safe return and reaffirming his unshakable belief that everything that happened, good or bad, was ordered by an omnipotent and just God: "I hope we will yet be able to damage our adversaries when they meet us, and that all will go right with us. That it should be so, we must implore the forgiveness of God for our sin, and the continuance of His blessings. There is nothing but His almighty power that can sustain us."

Even though he failed in his ultimate objective, Lee called the Gettysburg campaign a "general success" in his report to President Davis, thanks to "the guidance of the Most High." He added that, "though it did not win a victory . . . I still think if all things could have worked together it would have been accomplished." At the same time, there was a loud public outcry that Lee had failed to get a foothold in Pennsylvania. The general didn't care about public criticism, but if his departure could help Davis or help win the war, Lee offered to resign: "The general remedy for the want of success in a military commander is his removal. . . . I therefore, in all sincerity request Your Excellency to take measures to supply my place. I do this with the utmost earnestness because no one is more aware than myself of my inability for the duties of my position."

In a warm and personal reply, Davis reassured his commander: "Suppose, my dear friend, that I were to admit, with all their imperfections, the points which you present, where am I to find that new commander? To ask me to substitute you by some one in my judgment more fit to command, or who would possess more of the confidence of the army, or of the reflecting men of the country, is to demand an impossibility."

Lee, and many others after him, believed deep down that the seeds of frustration and failure at Gettysburg were sown when the man Lee called his good right arm was killed at Chancellorsville. Years later and a world away in the quiet woods of Lexington, Virginia, Lee confided to a riding companion, "If I had had Stonewall Jackson with me, so far as man can see, I should have won the battle of Gettysburg."

# SIXTEEN

## Our Duty to Live

IF THE OUTCOME at Gettysburg was debatable, the news from Vicksburg was not. On July 4, 1863, the day after Pickett's charge, Vicksburg fell at last to General U. S. Grant after forty-seven days. The whole Confederate West was now cut off. The army was losing ground in Tennessee. Wilmington, North Carolina, was the only Southern seaport that Lincoln had not yet shut tight.

With hard news on every front, Lee turned to God for relief. He and President Davis were convinced that God would withdraw His favor from a sinful and ungrateful people. Davis set August 21 as a national day of "fasting, humiliation, and prayer." On the thirteenth, Lee issued a general order suspending all but essential military duties that day and encouraging officers to stage "divine services." The order continued,

Soldiers! we have sinned against Almighty God. We have forgotten his signal mercies, and have cultivated a revengeful,
haughty, and boastful spirit. We have not remembered that the
defenders of a just cause should be pure in his eyes; and that
"our times are in his hands;" and we have relied too much on
our own arms for the achievement of our independence. God
is our only refuge and our strength. Let us humble ourselves
before Him. Let us confess our many sins, and beseech Him to
give us a higher courage, a purer patriotism, and more determined will; that He will convert the hearts of our enemies; that
He will hasten the time when war, with its sorrows and suf-
ferings, shall cease, and that He will give us a name and place
among the nations of the earth.

Lee kept up his sparring with Meade over the summer and into
the fall with little to show on either side, then settled into winter
quarters at his camp in Orange. The weather was brutal. Sentries
froze to death at their posts. Again Lee lived in his headquarters
tent, even though any one of the prosperous residents of Orange
would have welcomed him to a magnificent home. Montpelier,
once the estate of James Madison, and Meadowfarm, ancestral
seat of the Zachary Taylor clan, were only two of many plantations
that would have gladly entertained him with soft feather beds and
elegant meals served on fine linen. But Lee wintered with his men.
At least the general had a tent. The government had none for the
rank and file, who were on their own to build whatever huts they
could in order to survive until spring.

With the turn of the new year, 1864, Lee sent sixteen out of every hundred men home on rotating leave because he couldn't feed them. His repeated requests for more rations went unmet. In January the daily allotment was four ounces of bacon and a pint of cornmeal. Food was scarce and outrageously expensive everywhere in the South. An order of bread and butter in Richmond was a dollar fifty; a cup of coffee, three dollars.

Terrorizing the countryside had become a potent Union weapon. Meade's men destroyed homes and farm equipment, leaving helpless women and children without food. Farther west, General William T. Sherman ordered the complete destruction of Meridian, Mississippi, declaring afterward, "I have no hesitation in pronouncing the work as well done. Meridian . . . no longer exists."

Spring 1864 found the Confederate States more desperate than ever. Their resources were frayed to the last thread. The North meanwhile was preparing to strike the final blow. Lincoln wanted to win the war before the presidential election in November. Though the Union clearly had the upper hand, its people were tired of fighting and might vote for a Democrat running on a peace platform. Lincoln appointed U. S. Grant as general in chief and called for a fresh infusion of 700,000 soldiers. Grant lost no time getting to work. Where Meade or Hooker or McClellan had failed to press his advantage when he gained one, Grant would not hesitate. It was time for unlimited war. Relentlessly, ruthlessly, he would carry the fight in northern Virginia to the steps of the Confederate capitol until the rebels were crushed.

The first move in Virginia with Grant in charge came the morning of May 4, 1864, when Northern troops began crossing the Rapidan near Chancellorsville, headed for Richmond. Lee had to shift his army eastward from Orange to intercept them. To hold off more than 100,000 invaders (some sources place the figure as high as 140,000), Lee had about 62,000 underfed, under-equipped men. Looking for the most advantageous battleground, he picked a dense seventy-square-mile thicket between Orange and Chancellorsville called the Wilderness of Spotsylvania. There his men would have the cover of the forest and thick undergrowth that would also render the superior Northern artillery useless.

Preparing to go on the march Lee faced two major challenges. First, the roads that Ewell's and Hill's corps were traveling on, though generally parallel, veered far enough apart that Union troops could slip between the two. Second, Longstreet's men, who'd been west of Orange guarding a crucial railroad junction and had farther to march, were not yet on the field. By the after-noon of May 5, Lee decided not to wait any longer and sent Ewell and Hill to attack. The battle raged back and forth until after dark. Near the end of the day when it looked like the Federals would achieve a breakthrough, Lee called up the only reserves he had, 125 men from an Alabama battalion who were guarding prison-ers. The new troops came on with such shouting and commotion that in the heavy undergrowth and fading light, the enemy thought there were a lot more of them and pulled back for the night.

Longstreet's forces should have arrived around midnight, but at supper Lee got word that they wouldn't be there on time. When the battle opened the next morning, Confederates held the line as long as they could. By noon, Lee could see that without Longstreet, the battle was lost, and he ordered the supply wagons readied for retreat. At that moment members of Longstreet's lead brigade, eight hundred Texans under General John Bell Hood's command, crashed through the smoke and underbrush ready for action. Knowing there wasn't a moment to spare, Lee himself formed the men into a line and prepared to lead the charge. When the troops realized what he was about to do, they refused to advance until he went safely to the rear. Longstreet's forces firmed up the line and advanced, regaining ground lost earlier in the day and more, though Longstreet was badly wounded by friendly fire. Ewell's corps pushed forward as well and captured more than a thousand prisoners.

The following day, May 7, the two sides skirmished again before Grant withdrew. The big difference between Grant and his predecessors was that instead of falling back across the Rapidan to regroup as they would have done, Grant set out May 8 to march around the Confederates in the Wilderness and continue toward Richmond. Lee figured Grant's next step would be to attack the settlement at Spotsylvania Court House, about ten miles in the direction of the capital. He hurried his army there and had them dig a solid line of defensive earthworks in an arc north of the village.

Union troops arrived on May 9, and the fighting began. Both sides soon realized that the top of Lee's defensive arc, a salient known as the Mule Shoe, was a weak point in the defense. On the second day of battle, Federals broke through the line momentarily but were driven back. A lull in the action on May 11 gave Lee hope that his adversaries were going to withdraw as they had in the Wilderness. But early on the morning of the twelfth, Union infantry and artillery unleashed a massive assault on the Mule Shoe.

Again Lee came forward to lead his men, and again they ordered him back before they would advance. Rain overnight turned the battleground into a quagmire and fouled the gunpowder in many infantrymen's cartridges, making their firearms useless. The two sides crowded into the Mule Shoe locked in hand-to-hand combat, churning up mud so deep that wounded soldiers drowned in it. Men fought standing on layers of dead bodies.

Desperately trying to hold the enemy back, Lee ordered a new defensive line set at the bottom of the Mule Shoe. Around 3:00 a.m., May 13, the new position was ready, and the Confederates jumped behind it. There they held fast day after day through repeated attacks from Grant, who declared he would "fight it out on this line if it takes all summer." Against all odds the defenders hung on. At last on May 20, Grant pulled out, backing up north, then moving relentlessly southeast toward Richmond.

The Union general repeatedly fought to a standstill, then pulled out and moved southeast, closer to Richmond. Grant's method was time-consuming and costly, but that didn't matter to him because he had unlimited time and resources. Working an interior line, Lee could hold out indefinitely as long as he had enough men and supplies. He was still thinking ahead of Grant, still planning to attack at every opportunity and keep the advantage of surprise. But without a minimum level of troops and the tools of warfare, he was only delaying the inevitable.

By the first of June, Lee had withdrawn to the town of Cold Harbor southwest of the Pamunkey River, only about ten miles from Richmond. The opposing armies were now back where they'd been two years before, during the Peninsula campaign, when Lee had driven McClellan away from the capital. As a grim reminder, soldiers digging earthworks uncovered skeletons from the earlier battles.

With Richmond almost at his back and still outnumbered two to one, Lee built a masterpiece of defensive emplacements, an interconnected web of trenches reinforced with logs and protected by artillery in every direction. The battle at Cold Harbor began in earnest on June 1, when the attackers fell back with 2,200 casualties. The next day the Union army stood its ground without another offensive, and Lee took advantage of the pause to further strengthen his defenses. Grant then unleashed a massive attack on the morning of the third. It was a decision he regretted the rest of his life. Advancing before dawn through thick fog, their plan based on faulty reconnaissance, the Federals were cut down with almost no Confederate losses.

Grant's generals were furious with him for ordering an attack into so strong a position with such poor coordination. One Union soldier later recalled, "We felt it was murder, not war." When Grant pressed his commanders to exploit any opportunity, one of them insisted that further fighting was a "wanton waste of life." After staring at each other for days across no-man's-land while the wounded cried out for water, Union brigades finally gave up. For once the Confederates gave far more than they got, taking 4,500 casualties, including 83 killed, while inflicting more than 12,000 losses with more than 1,800 dead.

Cold Harbor convinced Grant that he wouldn't defeat Lee soon, if ever, by direct engagement in spite of overwhelming numbers. Lee kept eking out standoffs or victories though he had almost nothing to work with. Grant changed his strategy to attack the Confederacy's weakest point: transportation and supply.

On June 14, with the enemy trenches empty and the bluecoats gone, Lee informed President Davis that Grant "may be sending troops up the James River with the view of getting possession of Petersburg before we can reinforce it." It was a serious development. Petersburg was south of Richmond on the Appomattox, a tributary of the James, and was arguably the most important city in the Confederate States for supplying the capital with food and everything else. Three railroads converged there and went north to the city twenty miles away. If Petersburg were captured and the railroad destroyed, Richmond would starve.

A small force of 2,500 under irascible General Henry Wise manned a line of defensive earthworks stretching for ten miles east of Petersburg. All he had for reinforcements was the Home Guard, a defense militia of teenage boys, old men, and wounded soldiers from the hospitals. Lee sent General P. G. T. Beauregard to support Petersburg until Lee could get there in force.

To stop the Federals, Lee would have to defend trenches and fortifications that ran from south of Petersburg up to Richmond and west across the rail lines going north out of town—twenty-six miles in all. Beauregard arrived in time to prevent a Union victory, then held off 50,000 troops with a force of 14,000 while the defensive lines were strengthened. The next six weeks were essentially a stalemate. It wasn't a siege exactly because the railroads continued to run. Now Grant's impatience was showing. He knew from his experience at Vicksburg that long waits were terrible for troop morale. The delay was also politically inconvenient for Lincoln.

Impossibly occupied as he was, Lee wrote his wife a tender note on June 30, their wedding anniversary:

> Do you recollect what a happy day thirty-three years ago this was? How many hopes and pleasures it gave birth to? God has been very merciful and kind to us and how thankless and sinful I have been. I pray that He may continue His mercies and blessings to us, and give us a little peace and rest together in this world, and finally gather us and all He has given us around His throne in the world to come.

Around that time, Henry Pleasants, a mining engineer before the war and now a lieutenant colonel commanding the Forty-eighth Pennsylvania Infantry, went to Grant with an idea for relieving the stalemate. He proposed digging a tunnel under the Confederate line, filling it with explosives, blowing a hole in the enemy's position, then surging in to take Petersburg. With Grant's approval, the tunnel was completed and filled with eight thousand pounds of gunpowder. A little before 5:00 a.m. on July 30, a massive explosion blew a hole in the line thirty feet deep, nearly a hundred feet wide, and killed three hundred or more Confederates.

Fortunately for Lee and his men, the Union follow-up was badly organized. A division of U.S. Colored Troops had been specially trained to move forward after the explosion. But at the last minute, fearing the political fallout if anything went wrong and black soldiers got hurt, General Meade (still in the field, though answering to Grant) insisted that the Colored Troops remain in reserve. The replacement division was chosen by lot; on the day of battle, its commander was drunk. Having no idea what to do, the men climbed into the crater without ladders for climbing out, making them target practice for the Confederates, who could stand at the rim and fire, like shooting fish in a barrel. Grant called it "the saddest affair I have witnessed in the war."

Lee advised Davis on September 2 that he thought it was time to bring Southern blacks into the fight as teamsters, cooks, blacksmiths, tradesmen, and laborers. "It seems to me that we must choose between employing negroes ourselves, and having them employed against us," he wrote. That same day, General William Sherman destroyed Atlanta. The decisive effort meant that Lincoln was sure to be reelected and that the Deep South was lost.

The last action of 1864 around Petersburg was a Union blow against the Weldon Railroad, the track that headed south to Wilmington. By the time the Confederates got to the scene, the freezing attackers had returned to their camp. Elsewhere the news continued bleak. When General John Bell Hood led a desperate attempt to recapture Nashville in mid-December, he watched his remnants of a command disintegrate. Christmas week, General Sherman carried his reign of destruction to Savannah and set his sights on Charleston, where the whole business had begun.

Mrs. Lee left Richmond for Bremo, a still-quiet plantation eighty miles to the west owned by a family friend, Dr. Charles Cocke. Arlington had been confiscated and turned into a graveyard. Montgomery Meigs, Lee's traveling companion in St. Louis years ago, had been appointed quartermaster general of the U.S. Army. Secretary of War Stanton decided to make Arlington a national cemetery and left it up to Meigs to handle the details.

Considering General Lee a traitor, Meigs ordered graves dug encircling the mansion and as close to it as possible. When the first soldiers there were buried half a mile from the house near the old slave graveyard, Meigs angrily ordered them dug up and reinterred in "the land immediately surrounding the Arlington Mansion."

In January 1865, General Lee endorsed legislation to bring black soldiers into the ranks in exchange for their freedom. "My own opinion is that we should employ them without delay," he explained. "I believe that with proper regulation they can be made efficient soldiers."

The sad fact was that nothing could preserve the Confederate States of America. On January 15, Union forces occupied Wilmington, closing the last Southern port. Three weeks later, on February 6, Robert E. Lee was appointed general in chief, theoretically freeing him from the endless political and staffing disasters that had so hampered him. Finally he could act without Davis looking over his shoulder. But it was too late. With Wilmington taken and the Shenandoah Valley in ruins, Atlanta lost, Tennessee lost, and the Mississippi River occupied, there was no way for the Confederacy to hold on. As a commander who always felt for and looked after his men, Lee knew the time had come to consider terms for ending the war.

Just before Lee's appointment, on February 3, Lincoln and his secretary of state, William Seward, met secretly with Confederate representatives to discuss the prospect of peace. As Lee feared, Lincoln would consider a truce only if the rebel states rejoined the Union and slavery were abolished; the Confederacy could not continue. Hearing the news, President Davis declared that

Lincoln's decisions would inspire the people to fight even harder. Lee knew better: no matter how brave his men's hearts were, their bodies were broken beyond hope. Lee currently had about 65,000 tattered men of all arms in the field against 280,000 Federals.

With Davis's permission, General Lee sent Grant a letter on March 2, explaining that he was "authorized to do whatever the result of the proposed interview may render necessary or advisable" to reach an agreement for ending the war. Grant turned him down, saying he had no authority to act on Lee's offer. It may be that Lee would have tried again on the basis of rejoining the Union, but President Davis was unalterably opposed to the idea.

Lee did his duty to the end, mounting an offensive at Fort Stedman, a point in the Union works east of Petersburg and close to Confederate defenses. The Southern soldiers actually broke through enemy lines but fell back for lack of support. Some attackers were captured or wounded when they stopped to eat food off the plentiful supply wagons. On April 1, after more than nine months outside Petersburg, Grant cut the tracks of the South Side Railroad while the leader of the Confederate forces there, General Pickett, was away at a shad bake. His most important line of supply and escape gone, Lee withdrew his meager forces and fell back. The next day Union soldiers poured through the lines, and at dawn on April 3, Petersburg surrendered. Richmond fell before sunset.

President Davis, his cabinet, government records, and all the gold bullion in the treasury left the capital by train for Danville to the west, where they would establish a new seat of government. Lee made plans to follow them, but without food his men simply could not go on. His soldiers were now eating corn intended for the livestock. As draft horses died of exhaustion and starvation in their traces, artillerymen broke up their wagon wheels for firewood. The night of April 7, Lee received a note from Grant asking for the surrender of his army to shift from Grant "the responsibility of any effusion of blood." Lee replied that he didn't share Grant's views of "the hopelessness of further resistance," but agreed with Grant's desire to avoid useless bloodshed. He asked what terms of surrender Grant would offer.

Grant replied, "Peace being my great desire, there is but one condition I would insist upon, viz, that the men and officers should be disqualified for taking up arms again against the Government of the United States until properly exchanged."

Before sunrise on April 9, 1865, Lee rose and put on his full dress uniform, complete with red silk sash and ceremonial sword. Seeing onlookers' surprise, Lee explained that he expected to be General Grant's prisoner and wanted to look his best. Someone wondered aloud what history would say about a Confederate surrender.

"I know they will say hard things of us," Lee admitted. "They will not understand how we were overwhelmed by numbers. But that is not the question. The question is: Is it right to surrender this army? If it is right, then I will take all the responsibility." Witnesses thought he would break down, but he managed to hold his composure. He declared that he would rather die than surrender and that he had "only to ride along the line and all will be over."

In that case, why not ride into enemy fire and end it all without the agony of defeat? As quickly as Lee had raised the question, he answered it: "But it is our duty to live. What will become of the women and children of the South if we are not here to protect them?"

Offered the choice of meeting places, Lee sent an aide to find a suitable spot. The place was the home of the McLean family at the settlement of Appomattox Court House. The two generals in chief agreed that the rebels would turn over their weapons and military supplies, with officers allowed to keep their horses, side-arms, and personal baggage. When Lee explained that enlisted soldiers had supplied their own horses and would need them for spring planting, Grant agreed to that too.

Lee asked if Grant would take the thousand Federal prisoners he had, since all he could feed them was parched corn. Grant said he would, and he offered to send Lee 25,000 food rations, which Lee gratefully accepted. Grant wrote out the agreement in pencil and had it copied in ink, and the two men signed it. As Lee rode away, Grant lifted his hat, and his staff followed suit. Lee lifted his hat in reply.

Riding back to his lines, the general was surrounded by men shocked at his expression. They waited for him to speak, but it was a moment before he could get the words out. "Men," he said in a low voice the crowd strained to hear, "we have fought the war together and I have done the best I could for you. You will all be paroled and go to your homes until exchanged." He couldn't say any more. His eyes filled with tears as his lips silently formed one last word.

*Good-bye.*

# SEVENTEEN

# An Affectionate Farewell

L E E  R O D E  T O  a quiet spot in an apple orchard, dismounted, and walked up and down alone. Those who watched him from a distance said that he "began to feel the reaction" of the day's events, that his legendary self-control was "at last completely broken." Whether he screamed, ranted, bawled, or stared into space, none of them recorded. But when he rode back to his headquarters in the failing afternoon light, tears were streaming down his cheeks. A crowd of soldiers waited in front of his tent to greet him, and when he dismounted, they raised a loud cheer, many of them sobbing like children. Lee stood before them, still unable to speak, took off his hat to acknowledge their greetings, paused a moment, and went inside.

In his last official address to his men, General Order No. 9, dated April 10, 1865, he praised their "unsurpassed courage and fortitude," but said that any further resistance would be a "useless sacrifice.... With an unceasing admiration of your constancy and devotion to your Country, and a grateful remembrance of your kind and generous consideration for myself, I bid you all an affectionate farewell."

Four days later, Robert and Rooney (who had been imprisoned in New York, exchanged in early 1864 for a Union general, and who had recovered from his wound) went together to Richmond. The city was a charred ruin, destroyed by fires set during the Confederate retreat. Bridges across the James were burned so that temporary boards over Union pontoons were the only way in. Gathering a crowd as they walked, the two arrived at 707 East Franklin Street and went inside. Well-disciplined Union soldiers had taken over the city and restored order. A sentry was posted in front of Lee's house to make sure he wasn't disturbed. Mrs. Lee sent him breakfast every morning on a silver tray.

Lee graciously entertained a steady stream of admirers, both Northern and Southern. Visitors brought food, supplies, and offers of financial assistance. What he really needed, his outspoken daughter Mary declared, was a way to earn a living. He had been a soldier all his life, and now that career was over. Though the economy of the South was completely destroyed, Lee would never leave his homeland.

There was also the question of his political status. Lee rightly assumed that according to the terms of surrender, no Southern soldier would be prosecuted by the United States government. President Lincoln, shot by a deranged actor named John Wilkes

Booth, had died the day that Lee arrived in Richmond, but President Andrew Johnson seemed ready to welcome the defeated Southerners as returning brothers and not conquered enemies. The new president's attitude didn't prevent U.S. District Judge John C. Underwood from calling on a grand jury to indict Lee and others for treason. Lee applied for a pardon contingent on his not being indicted, and he wrote General Grant for clarification. "I am ready to meet any charges that may be preferred against me, and do not wish to avoid trial," he explained. "But if I am correct as to the protection granted by my parole, and am not to be prosecuted, I desire to comply with the provisions of the President's proclamation, and, therefore, inclose the required application." He enclosed the parole document that he and six staff officers had signed at Appomattox on April 9.

Lee was never indicted. Later, on October 2, he signed and submitted the required Amnesty Oath to "abide by and faithfully support all laws and proclamations which have been made during the existing rebellion with reference to the emancipation of slaves, so help me God." However, Lee never received acknowledgment of his application, and no pardon was granted. (Secretary of State William Seward evidently gave Lee's oath to a friend as a souvenir, who left it in a drawer. It was discovered in 1970, and Lee's pardon was signed by President Gerald Ford in 1975.)

Early in the summer of 1865, Lee accepted an offer from Mrs. Elizabeth Cocke, relations of the Cockes of Bremo Plantation, to live at Derwent, a modest house near her own Oakland Plantation on the James River. The home was small—two rooms and a hall downstairs plus two rooms and a hall up—but surrounded by three thousand quiet acres where Lee could escape the endless stream of visitors in Richmond and think about his future. He considered writing a memoir of the war as a way to honor the men who had served. Lee contacted some of his generals and staff, encouraging them to write what they remembered and send it to him. Many of his records and notes had been lost or burned in the mad dash to evacuate Petersburg and Richmond, but perhaps he could reconstitute some of them.

During this brief season of calm, a visitor brought Lee a proposition. John W. Brockenbrough, rector of Washington College in Lexington, Virginia, called out of the blue to say that the college trustees had unanimously elected him its president at a salary of fifteen hundred dollars per year, plus a house and garden and a commission on tuition. Founded in 1749, the school was facing hard times in the aftermath of the war. Buildings had been ransacked, and the library and science laboratory were destroyed. Impoverished families struggled to find seventy-five dollars for annual tuition. The school's trustees hoped Lee could help them rebuild. Lee was afraid that questions about his amnesty and the scorn some people held for former Confederates might produce "a feeling of hostility" that would "cause injury to an Institution which it would be my highest desire to advance." He also said he didn't have the strength to teach classes. When the trustees assured him he would not have to teach, he accepted their offer.

Lee and the college moved quickly to be ready for the start of the fall term. At the end of his first week in Lexington, he wrote to Mary, "Life is indeed gliding away and I have nothing of good to show for mine that is past. I pray I may be spared to accomplish something for the benefit of mankind and the honor of God."

Lee believed that Washington College was the door God had opened for him when the Confederacy went down in defeat. It was his chance to help rebuild the broken South, and he put everything he had into the task. Mrs. Lee, accompanied by her children Rob and Mildred, arrived on December 2, as soon as their house on campus was ready. Agnes, who was away at a wedding, would join them later. Custis soon took a teaching position at the college and lived in the house as well. The general had been able to collect the Mount Vernon drapes and Arlington carpets stored away before the war, the carpets folded under at the edges to fit in the much smaller rooms. The only fully furnished room was Mrs. Lee's bedroom. The furniture was commissioned by Mrs. Cocke and built by a one-armed Confederate veteran. Lee had recovered the family silver, sent to Lexington years before and buried on the grounds of Virginia Military Institute, but it still needed to be washed and polished. So they ate their first meal, a hearty breakfast cooked by the mathematics teacher's wife, with Robert's well-worn camp kit.

Another buried treasure was less durable than silver. George Washington's personal and family papers, also buried for safekeeping, were mildewed and rotted beyond saving. Mary herself burned them in the fireplace, near tears as she "had to commit to the flames papers that had been cherished for nearly a century."

Admirers constantly asked for Lee's remembrances of the war or views about various aspects of it. For all he had endured and lost, Lee held fast to his belief in states' rights. When Sir John

Dalberg-Acton, later Lord Acton, wrote requesting his views on the American political landscape, the general answered that he considered "the preservation of the constitutional power of the General Government to be the foundation of our peace and safety at home and abroad." But this foundation depended on "the rights and authority reserved in the states," which were "the safeguard to the continuance of a free government. I consider . . . the consolidation of the states into one vast republic, sure to be aggressive abroad and despotic at home, to be the precursor of that ruin which has overwhelmed all those that have preceded it."

By the end of the school year, Lee's presence had given beleaguered Washington College a national reputation. The school took in more than $100,000, including $15,000 from Cyrus McCormick, inventor of the mechanical reaper. The trustees doubled Lee's salary to $3,000, agreed to build a new campus chapel, and planned a spacious new home for his family designed to accommodate Mrs. Lee's wheelchair. The arthritis she endured for decades had become so painful and debilitating that she could no longer take even a step. Rob carried her to her coach and up the stairs, just as Robert had carried his mother.

Robert E. Lee considered himself "very retired" from military and political matters, but was nevertheless called before a congressional committee considering whether former Confederate states could send senators and representatives to a postwar Congress. Lee appeared on February 17, 1866, as one of those "at the head of rebellion." He said little, answering in as few words as possible. In this he was taking his own advice, given in a letter to the wife of Jefferson Davis, that "silence and patience" were the surest roads to reconciliation. During his visit to Washington, Lee attracted cheering crowds everywhere he went.

As president of Washington College, Lee did everything he could to prepare the next generation of Southern men. He expanded the curriculum and, more important, introduced the honor system. Faculty members no longer made unannounced visits to the dormitories, and students were discouraged from telling on each other. If a student was guilty of bad behavior, Lee expected him to report it himself. When a new arrival once asked for a copy of the school's rulebook, Lee explained, "We have no printed rules. We have but one rule here, and that is that every student must be a gentleman."

In four years Lee raised enrollment from about fifty to more than four hundred and put the school on solid financial footing. He seldom took a vacation, even though his heart ailment continued and his wife was completely unable to walk. In the spring of 1867 the family took a trip to the famous mineral baths at White Sulphur Springs, now in West Virginia, where an elegant hotel built in 1854 had reopened for the first time since the war. The general was the center of attention wherever he went, but his favorite pastime was riding Traveller through the mountains alone.

That fall Lee and Custis traveled to nearby Petersburg for the happy occasion of Rooney's marriage. His first wife and two children had died of sickness during the war, and he was marrying again. Robert sent all the details in letters home to Mary.

At the hotel in Richmond, Lee was swamped by well-wishers and former members of his command. On the short train ride to Petersburg he passed throngs of people who stood waving beside the track. A musical band of veterans played for him at a stop and then climbed aboard to shake his hand. In Petersburg a crowd gathered outside the church three hours before the wedding to watch the general walk in.

From the time he left for the springs until he returned from a round of visits after Rooney's wedding, Lee was absent from Washington College for five months, the longest he'd ever been away. The trip helped change his mind about the progress of recovery in the South. On his journey to Richmond and Petersburg he had seen people at work, factories rebuilt, goods for sale in the stores, and broad signs of recovery. In a letter to Rooney he reported, "When I saw the cheerfulness with which the people were working to restore their condition, and witnessed the comforts with which they were surrounded, a load of sorrow which had been pressing upon me for years was lifted from my heart." His agony at the thought of failing millions of Southerners who'd looked to him for leadership was gone at last.

The Republicans nominated U. S. Grant as their presidential candidate for the election of 1868. In response there was a wave of support to put Robert E. Lee on the Democratic ticket. No less than the *New York Herald Tribune* declared, "General R. E. Lee . . . is one in whom the military genius of this nation finds its fullest development . . . [who,] with a handful of men whom he had moulded into an army, baffled our greater Northern armies for four years; and when opposed by Grant was only worn down by that solid strategy of stupidity that accomplishes its object by mere weight."

Lee made no public response to the suggestion, believing no doubt he was too busy, too poorly qualified, and too tired for the job. After another round of summer visits to the hot springs, Lee returned for the start of the fall term in September more exhausted than ever. His youngest daughter, Mildred, had caught typhoid fever, and Mrs. Lee couldn't tend her because she couldn't climb the stairs. The general watched Milly at night; she couldn't fall asleep unless her father was holding her hand.

Christmas 1868 was one of the most joyous in years. Everyone in the family except Rooney was in Lexington. Mildred, who'd made a remarkable recovery, jokingly recited a long list of Christmas presents she expected. By Christmas morning, her father had gotten her every one of them. He also rode around the neighborhood and delivered presents to every child. Mrs. Lee had made dolls with dresses cut from her old ball gowns for the girls, and mittens or braided riding whips for the boys.

The new year was a mixed blessing to the general and his family. On May 31, the trustees handed Lee the keys to a spacious new president's house. It was nearly twice the size of the old one, with running water, central heat, and a wide verandah on three sides with long French windows giving Mary access from all the front rooms in her wheelchair.

For all the new home's conveniences, Mary always longed for Arlington. Lee had little hope of reclaiming the estate but thought he might recover some of the furnishings confiscated by the Federals. As one of his last acts as president before Grant's inauguration, Andrew Johnson gained cabinet approval to return all remaining Arlington property to Mrs. Lee. Overjoyed, she sent a cousin in Washington to claim the items. But when a notice of the plan was published, John A. Logan, former Union general, current member of the U.S. House of Representative, and rabid reconstructionist, was able to stop it. On the night of March 3, less than twenty-four hours before the end of Johnson's presidency, a congressional report found that the belongings were in fact "the property of the Father of his country, and as such are the property of the whole people and should not be committed to the custody of any one person, much less a rebel like General Lee." To do so was "an insult to the loyal people of the United States." The president's order was countermanded.

Lee took this ironic, public, and flagrant insult without complaint, humbly observing that the belongings

> were valuable to [my wife] as having belonged to her great-grandmother, and having been bequeathed to her by her father. But as the country desires them, she must give them up. I hope their presence at the capital will keep in the remembrance of all Americans the principles and virtues of Washington.
>
> From what I have learned, a great many things formerly belonging to General Washington . . . in the shape of books, furniture, camp equipage, etc., were carried away by individuals and are now scattered over the land. I hope the possessors appreciate them and may imitate the example of their original owner, whose conduct must at times be brought to their recollection by these silent monitors. In this way, they will accomplish good to the country.

Lee was technically still executor of his father-in-law's estate and hoped some of the property would be returned so he could raise the $40,000 that Mr. Custis had promised his granddaughters. It would not happen in Lee's lifetime. (After his parents' deaths, Custis continued pressing the case. Finally in 1882 the U.S. Supreme Court ruled that Arlington had been illegally confiscated and that Custis Lee was the rightful owner. Unwilling to live surrounded by tens of thousands of military graves, Custis sold Arlington to the U.S. government for $150,000, part of which he used to pay his sisters' legacies. Washington's remaining belongings were returned to the family by executive order of President William McKinley in 1901.)

In May, after Grant took office, Lee was in Baltimore on behalf of a group of men trying to build a rail line to Lexington, and he stopped for a courtesy call on his former adversary. There is no record of their private conversation, which lasted about fifteen minutes; all that is known of the meeting is that they shook hands when they met and when they parted. It was the only time after Appomattox that the two men met.

By Christmas 1869, Lee's energy was steadily declining and his chest pains getting worse and more frequent. Any sudden movement caused sharp pains and shortness of breath. He told the trustees that he couldn't do his job anymore and that it was time for him to retire. They encouraged him to take a leave of absence to travel instead, to rest and restore his strength. At first he insisted he felt too bad to travel, but finally agreed to take two months off for a trip South in order not to appear "obstinate, if not perverse" to those "so interested in my recovery."

Once he made up his mind to go, he planned a valedictory journey to all the places he wanted to see and didn't expect to see again. Agnes traveled with him. They left Lexington by canal boat for Richmond on March 24, 1870. Three days later they began a railroad odyssey, first to Warrenton Springs to visit Annie's grave, then on to Savannah. The night of March 29, Lee was awakened by crowds in Raleigh cheering, "Lee! Lee!" As word spread that General Lee was on the way, crowds grew exponentially at every stop. Mothers held up their babies named Robert E. Lee. At Columbia, South Carolina, businesses closed and the whole city waited at the station in driving rain.

"Why should they care to see me?" he asked Agnes. "I'm only a poor old Confederate."

During ten days in Savannah, Lee visited his father's grave on Cumberland Island and met with many comrades who were now company presidents, newspaper publishers, lawyers, and foreign ambassadors. Lee went by boat to Jacksonville, Florida, where another huge crowd awaited. So many tried to rush aboard that the vessel was almost swamped. Lee appeared on deck to satisfy the crowd, and to the amazement of onlookers, the throng went completely silent. As the *Jacksonville Union* reported, "The very silence of the multitude spoke a deeper feeling than the loudest huzzas could have expressed."

The adulation continued every place he went: an honor guard of cadets at Wilmington, an artillery salute in Portsmouth, dinners and receptions everywhere. On May 10 he arrived at Shirley, which seemed almost untouched by four years of war. Lee relished two quiet days there, much of which he spent sitting in the large elegant parlor where his parents were married. His most frequent companions were some of the Hill grandchildren, whose company he adored. He gave them autographed pictures and left them with an impression of "great dignity and kindness." One of them remembered years later, "We regarded him with the greatest veneration. We had heard of God, but here was General Lee!"

On the afternoon of Wednesday, September 28, 1870, Lee left his house on campus for a short walk through the rain to a vestry meeting at Grace Episcopal Church. There they talked, among other things, about the fact that the fund for the pastor's salary was fifty-five dollars short. Lee volunteered to pay it. Arriving home at 7:30, later than usual for vestry nights, Lee hung up his hat and coat in his bedroom and went into the dining room where his wife, Agnes, and Mildred waited on him to serve tea. Mrs. Lee was sewing.

"You have kept us waiting a long time," she chided gently. What have you been doing?"

In silence, Lee stood at the head of the table to say grace but then sat without speaking.

"You look very tired," Mary said. "Let me pour you a cup of tea."

He didn't respond, and his face had a strange look. She sent for the doctor, who had been at the same vestry meeting, and he and Custis got Lee undressed and into his bed. After sleeping almost nonstop for two days and nights, the general seemed a little more aware. Doctors gave him medicine and bled him, confident at first he would recover. "He did not speak except a few words occasionally," Mary wrote to a cousin, "but always greeted me with an outstretched hand & kindly pressure, took his food with some pleasure & we vainly thought was getting on comfortably."

Lee never rose again from his bed. Biographers agree that Lee seemed to be dreaming of the war in his last moments. "Tell Hill he must come up," he said, and finally, "Strike the tent." Mary mentioned nothing of any last words in a letter written October 12, the day Lee died, only that in the end he "seemed to pass away gently." She continued:

> We all prayed God so fervently to prolong a life so important to his family & country, but *He* in His mysterious Providence thought best to call him to those mansions of rest which He has prepared for those who love and serve Him & oh, what rest to his toilsome & eventful life. . . .
>
> I pray that his noble example may stimulate our youth to a course of uprightness which never wavered from the path of duty at any sacrifice or ease or pleasure, & so long too has the will of God been the guiding star of his actions. . . .
>
> I have never so truly felt the purity of his character as now when I have nothing left me but its memory, a memory which I know will be cherished in many hearts besides my own.

Mary did not attend the funeral at the college chapel. Having to deal with a crush of people while she was in her wheelchair was more than she could bear. Instead she stayed at home, read her husband's letters written over nearly forty years, and listened to the sounds of his favorite hymn flowing from the open windows of the chapel into her room:

How firm a foundation, ye saints of the Lord,
  Is laid for your faith in His excellent Word!
What more can He say than to you He has said,
  To you who for refuge to Jesus have fled?

Robert E. Lee's earthly remains were placed in a crypt under the chapel for the time being, though the college trustees told his widow they would move them anywhere she wished. Mary could think of no better place than under the chapel of the college that would raise up a new generation of leaders for the South.

Near the end, she and Robert had talked of faith and salvation, and characteristically, genuinely, he wondered whether he had made the grade. Had he done his duty? She wrote so tenderly of the moment, a fitting final image made of love and loss and peace. It was an image worthy of a true warrior and gentleman:

"So humble was he as a Christian that he said not long ago to me he wished he felt sure of his acceptance. I said all who love & trust in the Savior need not fear. He did not reply, but a more upright & conscientious Christian never lived."

The house at 707 East Franklin in where Mary Custis Lee waited out the war, and were General Lee joined her after hostilities ended. The building narrowly escaped the fire that destroyed much of the city in the aftermath of the Confederate surrender.

General Lee (far right) with other veterans at White Sulphur Springs, West Virginia c. 1867. Lee was taking a much-needed rest from duties as president of Washington College in Lexington, Virginia.

A portrait from 1870, the year of Lee's death, shows a weary yet still regal face and carriage.

Death mask of General Robert E. Lee.

Funeral of General Lee at the Washington University chapel. Mrs. Lee was too ill to attend, but heard the hymns from her home on campus. In time the entire Lee family came to rest at the chapel, the last member (Annie, who had been buried at Warrenton Springs in 1862) reinterred in 1994.

# Legacy

THE EARLIEST HISTORICAL record of Robert E. Lee describes an exceptional boy, and an aura of superiority seemed to surround his life from first to last. He was marked for leadership and responsibility before his teenage years, helping his invalid mother run the household after his father abandoned the family and his oldest brother left for Harvard. He was a standout at West Point: a diligent student, a patient tutor to underclassmen, flawless in executing orders, without a demerit in four years of school. The mayor of St. Louis praised him for his work supervising a military engineering project there: Lee was courteous, efficient, humble, reliable, and scrupulously honest. General-in-chief Winfield Scott singled him out for special attention after the Mexican War for his resourcefulness and bravery. When

President Buchanan needed a trusted and capable officer on short notice to put down a slave rebellion at Harpers Ferry, Lee got the call. When President Lincoln raised an enormous army in hopes of forestalling civil war, he asked Lee to command it. When the Confederacy seceded, they saw Lee as the only soldier to lead their forces. When Washington College made their plans to rebuild from the ruins, Lee was their choice as the man to bring them back from the brink of collapse.

Lee's leadership gift was that he could inspire men to go on when going seemed impossible, to dig deep within themselves for the will to endure. He demonstrated this power himself as a scout in Mexico, working around the clock to plan and coordinate the final assault on Mexico City. He inspired it in civilian laborers of St. Louis who worked under the baking sun enveloped in clouds of mosquitoes. He infused Confederate soldiers with the stamina and drive to march barefoot in January snow, to live on cattle feed, to stand fast long after they should have given up in honor of a cause long lost.

This inspiration derived from a superhuman—some would say supernatural, God-breathed—combination of ability, characteristics, and personality traits. For one, R. E. Lee looked like a leader. He was tall, handsome, always impeccably dressed and groomed (fine uniforms seemed his only indulgence), with superb posture, carriage, and horsemanship. For another, he accepted great responsibility without flinching: he cared for his mother, tutored fellow cadets, directed construction projects, led armies he knew had no chance of victory, assumed the presidency of a struggling college, was always willing to take charge and lead the way.

Lee was also personally brave, as his service in Mexico and

Virginia attest. Most important of all, Lee was all these things and deeply, genuinely humble. He worked along side the laborers in St. Louis when he didn't have to. He wintered with his men under miserable field conditions during the Civil War when any number of wealthy landowners would have been honored to host him. It was part of his job; he felt the obligation as their leader to share their burdens and discomforts. This humility was the key to Lee's leadership ability. Men worked harder for him out of respect and admiration than they ever would have out of obligation or fear, or even self-preservation. Soldiers under his command had for him the sincerest and purest form of *phileo*, the brotherly love that inspires one man to give his life for another on the battlefield, the power that fuses a "band of brothers"—comrades-in-arms bound together out of mutual respect, for mutual survival and sacrifice; the power that made Pickett's Charge possible along with all its iterations throughout history.

Yet another dimension of Lee is that for all the gravitas of his historical persona, during much of his life Lee was a fun-loving, witty fellow who enjoyed parties, conversation, theater, dancing, and innocent jesting. He loved life, relishing the good times with thanksgiving and accepting the bad with humble resignation.

All of these attributes Lee held lightly in his hand. In his view, it wasn't he that was infused with greatness or outsized ability. To him they were all gifts from God to an unworthy man. The good was God's providence; the bad, God's chastisement. This view appeared more strongly in his letters as he got older. He would say he was nothing but a "poor Confederate" with nothing to offer but whatever God had given him.

Uniquely gifted and highly praised as he was, Lee was not an infallible commander. His recurring flaw was to assume his subordinates had the same energy, bravery, resolve, and sense of self-sacrifice he did and then plan accordingly. When they didn't, his carefully wrought tactics yielded limited success or none at all. General Lee was too trusting, too willing to yield to others at crucial moments. He was too easily pesuaded to let commanders in the field modify his orders, believing they had a better grasp of the immediate situation. Time and again, most famously at Gettysburg, Lee was deferential when he should have been resolute, solicitous of others' opinions and feelings when he should have ignored them to follow the dictates of his own training, experience, and intuition. Variables on the battlefield are almost numberless, so that changing one of them may not have changed the outcome. However, if General Lee had been more forceful—even rude—at times, his inspired and meticulous plans may well have been executed more successfully, turning hard-fought defeats into victories and changing the course of American history.

Yet had that been the case, General Lee would not have become the General Lee so many admire today. Regardless of what sparked the Civil War and whether it was good or bad, Lee was a great leader in large part because he never abandoned his personal standards, never wavered from doing what he thought was right even in the face of inevitable, crushing, devastating consequences.

Seeing the storm ahead full well, Lee sailed into the middle of it because anything else would have been dishonorable, and therefore unthinkable.

# Bibliography

## Author's Note on Sources

Along with every other writer who attempts to paint an accurate and vibrant historical portrait of Robert E. Lee, I am particularly indebted to three sources.

First is *Personal Reminiscences of General Robert E. Lee* by J. William Jones, D.D. (1836-1909). Jones was a writer, preacher, theologian, and Confederate chaplain known as "the fighting parson," who served with General Lee during the war and was later secretary-treasurer of the Southern Historical Society. After Lee's death, the family chose Jones to write the general's biography and entrusted him with their store of letters to and from Lee. Jones incorporated them in his book, and they have subsequently been quoted and referenced in virtually every work about Lee published since. *Reminiscences* is a treasury of personal and family moments, many of them first-person eyewitness accounts. It is filled with private and professional details that breathe life into a historic figure.

Another essential source is *Recollections and Letters of General Robert E. Lee: By His Son*. Published in 1904 by Robert E. Lee, Jr. (1843-1914), this book is the other essential original source for details on Lee the soldier, educator, and family man. Together *Reminiscences* and *Recollections* are the wellspring for stories, quotations, and events that flow through every account of the general down through the years.

For every writer and reader who approaches the Lee saga, the shadow of Douglas Southall Freeman (1886-1953) looms large. His massive four-volume biography, *R. E. Lee*, won the Pulitzer Prize in 1935 and is an exhaustive account both scholarly and deeply felt. Freeman was also a newspaper editor in Richmond and won a second Pulitzer for his seven-volume biography of George Washington. The son of a Confederate soldier, Freeman as a boy lived down the street from General Jubal Early, one of Lee's finest officers and a lifelong defender of Southern secession. Freeman is accused in some quarters of being partisan himself and promoting the "lost cause" of the Confederacy in his chronicle of Lee's life. Nevertheless, *R. E. Lee* remains indispensable to all who seek to know this great and many-faceted man.

A useful and enriching source of more recent vintage is *The Civil War: A Narrative* by Shelby Foote (1916-2005), a three-volume history twenty years in the making, made famous by the

1990 PBS television special. While Foote's sweeping story is an all-encompassing panorama, his accounts of Lee extracted from official war records are an important addition to understanding Lee as a military leader.

# Acknowledgments

IT IS A daunting task to write about a historical figure who has already been chronicled so exhaustively, and whose every move is still subject to lively debate. I owe a debt of thanks to Joel Miller, Kristen Parrish, Heather Skelton, and Lisa Schmidt at Thomas Nelson for keeping me on track, with special gratitude to series editor Stephen Mansfield, whose knowledge of military writing in general and the Civil War in particular was a tremendous help.

I was ably assisted with photo research—and double quick, too—by Jamie Davis at the Virginia Historical Society; Patricia Hobbs, Lisa McCown, and Katie Gardner at Washington & Lee University; and Ann Drury Wellford at the Museum of the Confederacy. Readers who appreciate the dimension that photographs bring to Lee's story will applaud them along with me.

Thanks also to Andrew Wolgemuth, my friend and agent, for his signal role in keeping the nuts and bolts of the project in order so that the writer could concentrate on writing.

# About the Author

JOHN PERRY WAS born in Kentucky and after discharge from military service, graduated from Vanderbilt University. He also studied at University College, Oxford, England.

John began his career as an advertising copywriter in Houston, moving to Nashville in 1983, where he worked as a copywriter at Nashville-based advertising agencies. John was a founder of Wolf, Perry & Clark Music and American Network Radio (production and syndication of radio specials for Garth Brooks, Dolly Parton, and other country stars.). His work on a marketing project for a chain of bookstores led to an assignment for a publishing firm, which in turn led to John's transition from copywriter to author.

John is the biographer of *Sergeant Alvin York* and a Gold Medallion finalist for *Unshakable Faith*, a dual biography of

Booker T. Washington and George Washington Carver. He also is the author of *Lady of Arlington*, the biography of Mary Custis Lee, wife of Robert E. Lee and great-granddaughter of Martha Washington. John's most recent book, *Letters to God*, has been on the 2010 New York Times Best Seller list.

John now lives in Nashville.